10/00

*f*P

Coal *to* Cream

A black man's journey beyond color

to an affirmation

of race

Eugene Robinson

The Free Press

THE FREE PRESS
A Division of Simon & Schuster Inc.
1230 Avenue of the Americas
New York, NY 10020

THE FREE PRESS and colophon are trademarks
of Simon & Schuster Inc.

Designed by Carla Bolte

Manufactured in the United States of America

10   9   8   7   6   5   4   3   2   1

Library of Congress Cataloging-in-Publication Data

Robinson, Eugene, 1954–
     Coal to cream : a black man's journey beyond color to an affirmation
of race / by Eugene Robinson.
         p.   cm.
      1. Brazil—Race relations.   2. Blacks—Brazil—Race identity.
   3. Afro-Americans—Race identity.   4. United States—Race relations.
   5. Robinson, Eugene, 1954–   . I. Title.
   F2659.A1R58   1999   99-22037   CIP
   305.8'00981—dc21

ISBN 0-684-85722-7

To Avis, with love

Contents

The Girl From Ipanema

I'VE ALWAYS BEEN BLACK. THE SURPRISING NEWS THAT THERE was a place where I wasn't, necessarily, or at least didn't have to be, was imparted to me one hot summer's afternoon in Rio de Janeiro on the beach at Ipanema.

It was a special moment in my life, a time when suddenly I felt free as a bird and open to all sorts of new possibilities. I'd survived a tough, grinding dozen years as a newspaper reporter and editor in San Francisco and Washington, covering corruption and decay and despair and all the other cheery aspects of modern urban America, and was now embarked on a completely different path: I'd just been assigned as a foreign correspondent covering South America. Some people deal with burnout by changing jobs or houses or wives or buying a red convertible. I'd gone to an extreme, literally, by running off to the bottom of the world.

My base was Buenos Aires, where I'd installed my family in a nice suburban house with a pool. Green parrots woke us in the morning with their chatter; iridescent hummingbirds paused to sip from hibiscus blossoms that spilled off the balcony; we plucked pomegranates from the bush and lemons from our own little lemon tree — Argentina was a stunning and exotic new home. At least that's what my wife, Avis, told me: I was rarely there. My new job involved traveling essentially nonstop among the major cities of the continent. I lived mostly in hotel rooms, in airport departure lounges, and on the fleet of aging jets that airlines like Varig and Lan Chile and AeroPeru sent hurtling through the sky. I tried not to fly on planes that were older than I was.

Now I was taking my first real working visit to Brazil, and I'd looked up an American colleague who was living there temporarily. He invited me to spend a day of brilliant sun and gentle breeze with him and some of his friends, all Brazilians, at their usual spot on the beach.

One sure way of picking out the tourists in Rio, I quickly learned, was by the way they wandered aimlessly along the beaches, lacking destination or purpose, plopping down any old place, ogling the tanned bodies but otherwise providing themselves completely oblivious to the social landscape at their feet. Locals, on the other hand, headed straight for their niche sectors — areas of the beach favored by singles, gays, bodybuilders, soccer players, retirees, whatever — where they had arranged to meet their friends. Other Brazilians complain that gorgeous, dumb Rio has beaches instead of an intellectual life, but that's not quite true: The beaches *are* the venue for Rio's intellectual life, the local equivalent of smoke-filled cafés.

The sun shone hot that afternoon, the breeze blew balmy, and there I lay, amid a loose group of about a dozen young or youngish professionals—lawyers, journalists, a young woman who was trying to design and market her own line of string bikinis—all of us nearly nude, amply oiled, feeling the gritty warmth of the sand between our toes, languidly but earnestly discussing current events and the meaning of life. All around us was the wonderful Brazilian racial landscape, a mélange of blacks and browns and tans and taupes, of coppers and cinnamons and at least a dozen shades of beige.

Eventually, we got onto the subject of race. I was the one who raised it, trying to better understand the novel and amazing panorama I was seeing in Brazil. The conversation flowed into questions of what might be called racial taxonomy. Classification, in other words. Who, exactly, is considered black here? Who's white? Who's something else?

These weren't trivial questions. I could see that there were black people in Brazil, just like in the United States, and white people, although the proportions were obviously different. I knew that there had been a history of slavery and eventual emancipation. And yet I had the sense that the way people here thought of race was not at all the same way I thought of it. Even among my group at the beach, with the range of skin tones and hair types pretty much covering the whole spectrum, there was none of the obvious discomfort I had often felt whenever race came up in a mixed group in the States, none of the paralyzing fear of saying the wrong thing. Still, I wasn't making much sense of the inconsistent and contradictory things I was hearing. Race was important; race was trivial. There were tons of black people in Brazil; no, there really weren't that many. I wasn't getting it.

I decided to give up on theoretical classification and focus instead on the concept of race relations, which I figured would translate more easily. I turned to my colleague's Brazilian girlfriend, whose name I recall as Velma, and asked what it was really like being black in Brazil.

She answered with a look of genuine surprise.

"But I'm not," she said. "I'm not black."

She smiled at me as one smiles at a child who just doesn't understand, an isn't-he-precious kind of smile. But then I saw her quickly glance around at the others, making eye contact, and I had the sense she was somehow seeking to validate the declaration she had just made.

Velma had been born more than a thousand miles away, in the poor northeastern part of Brazil, the equivalent of our Deep South—a place where a plantation economy once flourished, where millions of African slaves had worked the fields, where slavery had persisted a full generation past the end of the American Civil War. It was obvious to me at first glance that Velma was primarily a descendant of those slaves. There was a lot of Indian in her, but mostly African. She was a small woman with long jet-black hair, flaring nostrils, high cheekbones, and brown skin at least a couple of shades darker than mine. It wasn't even a close call, in my book. But she was telling me she wasn't black.

I blurted out, "But you must be, Velma. I'm black, and you're as dark as I am."

She put her arm next to mine, to compare: Yes, she was darker. Positively, definitively darker.

"But this color isn't black," she said. "This isn't black at all."

Trapped on what she clearly saw as the wrong side of the color line I was trying to draw, Velma maintained flatly that as far as she was concerned, I wasn't really "black" either. I explained that in the United States I certainly was and always would be, and that so, in fact, would she. Velma found this hard to understand, and certainly wasn't about to accept it. She allowed that I might not be "white," but insisted that at the very least I fit well within the ill-defined parameters of *pardo*, which roughly means light-brown-skinned. "Black" was for her more of a description than a group designation, and it meant people with skin much darker than mine.

Or, of course, hers.

Others in our group, however, weren't quite so quick to settle on this classification. There were other factors. My hair, for example: It's kinky, clearly African, unarguably non-Caucasian. For some, kinky hair, in combination with skin as brown as mine, automatically equaled "black." Some thought that my physique—tall, slim, high-waisted—should somehow be factored in, that it was somehow an "African" physique. But foremost was the issue of my precise color, my own personal hue, which I'd never really thought about in this way—which I'd never really thought of as a color at all.

It's a kind of oakwood brown, with undertones more yellow than red. I seemed relatively lighter to some members of my informal college of taxonomists on the beach, relatively darker to others. Try as I might, I couldn't get this group of Brazilians to agree on what, racially speaking, I was. The conversation seemed to go in circles, and there was no way to get to the center.

Finally, exasperated, I turned again to Velma.

"If you're not black, what are you?" I asked. "You said I'm 'at least' *pardo*. Is that how you'd describe yourself?"

But I got no satisfaction. Rather than answer, she smiled, shrugged, and changed the subject. A while later, she and my American friend left.

After they'd gone, someone pointed out to me that Velma had long, straight hair, and that she also enjoyed the considerable status and income that came from her job as a lawyer. So naturally—and this was said as if it were the most natural thing in the world, though it made no sense at all to me—she called herself white.

White? A woman darker than me considering herself white? Not in my world. But of course I wasn't in my world anymore. I was in a world where race seemed to be indefinite, unfixed, imprecise—a world where, at least to some extent, race was what you made it.

Instead of what it made you.

That day on the beach was electrifying, eye-opening, liberating. I felt as if I'd just been let out of an airless little prison cell straight into the glorious space and hot sun and cooling zephyrs of Ipanema. In a way, I felt like I suppose Columbus must have felt. His business in sailing west had been to find a better route to the riches of the far east, and along the way he'd bumped into something unexpected, something far bigger and more significant, something life-changing. My business in coming to Brazil had been to write newspaper stories, and along the way I'd bumped into something unexpected, something big and life-changing, my own new world.

And if I'd been able to get my arms all the way around this new world, I'd have pulled it to me and given it a big sloppy kiss.

Chapter 1

Escape

IT WAS A LONG JOURNEY FROM WHERE I STARTED TO THAT BRAZILIAN beach. I got there by engineering an escape from the confines of my own skin—an escape from self, from family, from group, and above all from race.

I am a foreign correspondent by trade, and I was in Rio because the news had taken me there. But I also have a lot of other identities:

I am an African-American who once was black, once was a Negro, once was a colored boy.

I am a child of the segregated Deep South who came of age just as the civil rights movement changed everything.

I am a chronic integrator, sometimes by accident and sometimes by design, who since high school has always been either a black student at white schools or a black employee at white institutions.

I am a black man, the father of two black sons, in an era when black maleness in America is considered a deadly disease and those who suffer it are shunned like carriers of the bubonic plague.

I am a card-carrying member of the black middle class, which by definition means the stress of trying to live the good life on an adequate salary but with little or no underlying family wealth.

Because of all these things, I am a de facto mediator, a middleman. When I went to South America, I was at a point in my life when the feeling of being squeezed between worlds was particularly intense. I am also a writer, so I thought of my situation in terms of a writer's metaphor: I was like the tip of the pencil, the point where graphite meets paper, where black meets white. The part that is constantly ground into dust.

But this personal history explains only part of my reaction to Brazil. For the rest, I have to look back much further. Back a hundred years.

In the living room of the white clapboard house where I grew up, on the corner of Boulevard and Oak in Orangeburg, South Carolina, hang two old photographs, formal portraits taken around the turn of the century. One is of the gentleman who was the original owner and patriarch of the house, a man with flashing dark eyes, his skin very black, just this side of coal; the other is of a woman with dark hair and eyes but very light skin, almost like cream. They are Major John Hammond Fordham, my great-grandfather, and Louisa Gertrude Fordham, my great-grandmother, and their contrasting hues drew a set of borders for me in my early life, borders of race, identity, and color.

My grandmother, Sadie Fordham Smith, who lived to be ninety-eight and sassed the whole world until her dying day, used to tell stories about her father. She recalled how Major Fordham, "too slow and lazy and aristocratic to say good morning too loud," would stroll at a regal pace each day from his law office to the house for dinner, which was on the table at two in the afternoon. This was during the first few years to the new century, the major's ample middle years. On some days the sunlight would glint off his dark skin, highlighting his sharp cheekbones. On days when it rained he would approach through the gloom as slowly as ever, refusing to hurry one bit.

His wife, Louisa, would look down the street and see him coming on those rainy days. "Hammond!" she would yell, but he was oblivious. When he finally reached the house she would tell him he'd looked like a fool strolling through the rain.

"Not as much of a fool as I'd look running through it," my great-grandfather would reply. Then, removing his tailored jacket, now sopping and shapeless, he would make her exasperation complete with just the right touch of gall. "And now, Madam," he would say to his wife, "you may lay out fresh clothes for me."

In the house he ordered built for his family, the major installed a tiny window above the spot where he planned to install the piano—it was believed at the time, my grandmother explained, that pianos needed to breathe. I think of that window when I think of the parallels between his life and mine. Each of us was born into a time when a window of opportunity was opened, one that was excruciatingly narrow but still passable to those with enough luck, determination, and drive. He made it through; I have always been buoyed and burdened by the obligation to try.

Major Fordham was born a freeman in Charleston in 1856. He witnessed the end of slavery and the upheaval of the Civil War as a young child, and came of age during Reconstruction, a time when blacks in the South had unprecedented opportunities. I witnessed the end of Jim Crow segregation and the upheaval of the civil rights movement as a small child, and came of age at a time when society's doors, so long closed to people of color, were suddenly thrown open. Both of us were reasonably successful. And although our lives were separated by a hundred years, both of us had to deal with race as a central issue, for ourselves and the society around us. Much had changed in that time, but much had not.

Major Fordham's title came from his rank in the Carolina Light Infantry, where he once headed a "colored" brigade. He was a lawyer, a landowner, a politician, a public speaker of some renown, a man of culture and learning and great ambition. But when he walked down the street, most people saw none of that. They saw in him their own assumptions about what a coal-dark Negro in the deep South should be.

He was subservient. He was no better than chattel. He was inarticulate. He was stupid. He was buffoonish. He was a schemer. He was limited. He was a sexual predator, potentially, and had to be watched at all times lest he despoil a white woman, which he surely yearned to do. He was simple. He was always happy. He was a laborer who made his living with his hands and his back, and when those wore out he'd have nothing left. He was lazy. He was shiftless. He was a host for something savage, something that could never be fully trained, something that would keep him from ever having the discipline to offer anything of real value to America. He was physically powerful. He was intellectually inferior. He was a mortal threat.

He was, in fact, none of those things. His family knew that, his friends knew it, anyone who ever took more than five minutes to get to know him would have found it out. But of course most people didn't take that time—they didn't then, and they don't now.

Today, when people see me—I should say when they see us, meaning men who fit into that improbably wide spectrum we define as "black," roughly from the color of coal to the color of cream—they still assume, still pigeonhole, just as they did with the major. My teenage son Aaron, for example, can't just be seen as a teenager. When he puts on his clunky Timberland boots and his baggy jeans and his oversized sweatshirt and his knit cap, people see him as "thug" or "gangsta"—potentially, given his size, as "assailant." When he wears his prep-school uniform of khaki pants and button-down shirt, on the other hand, some people see him as "paragon," others as "token," still others as "sellout."

My young son Lowell can't go to school and just be a kid. He is a *black* kid, in a suburban American school system where black students are not assumed at first glance to be achievers. Teachers automatically see him as an "at-risk" child. They expect less of him than they should. Invariably they are surprised to learn he has a mother and a father at home, both of them professionals, both of them interested in his growth and development.

As for me, when I go into a fancy clothing store, if I'm dressed well, the salesmen assume I'm interested in the flashiest and most expensive items they have, since everybody knows that's what black men want to buy. If I'm dressed down, on the other hand, they give plainclothes security guards the "shoplifter" nod. When I encounter people professionally, I encounter a range of assumptions, depending on the situation: "slow learner," in which people speak very loudly and simply, as if I were hearing-impaired; "Super Negro," in which people lay out an obstacle course and expect me to run it for their amusement; and, of course, like Aaron, "token," "paragon," and "sellout."

There are other categories into which we're sorted: "gigolo," "jock," "Rasta," "Mandingo," "Superfly," "Slick Willie," dozens more. It's only natural, I suppose, to build up frameworks around people you encounter for the first time, to try to put them in some kind of context. But it's not natural to make those frameworks and that context exclusively racial in nature. In many people's eyes, I can never be just "the tall guy." I have to be "the tall *black* guy," and that adds another whole dimension.

People assume, from the addition of that one adjective, that they know a lot about me. They think they know a lot about my personal history, about my family life, about my taste in music, about my attitudes toward women, about my politics. Some people think they know a lot about my intelligence and even my virility. These prejudgments are tempered by specifics: If "the tall black guy" were delivering a lecture on U.S. foreign policy, say, then the intelligence assumption would be modified. But the assumptions are almost never completely eradicated. People dump them on me—on all of us—like so much extra baggage, an awful lot of weight to have to lug through life. I've always resented it. More than that: It has always made me angry, not the kind of anger that boils over but the kind that simmers and stews, the kind that ultimately poisons.

A newspaper story of the day called my great-grandfather one of the state's "most prominent colored men. By his own efforts and perseverance he has overcome all obstacles and has come to the front, respected, esteemed and admired by his legion of friends . . . a progressive man and an honorable, upright citizen."

Substitute "black" for "colored" and that could be a quote from my own obituary, if I'm lucky.

OVER THE YEARS, I'd grown weary of dealing with what white people thought they knew about me. More than weary: I was sick to death of it. But that wasn't the proximate reason for my escape to the tango parlors of Buenos Aires and the sands of Rio. The thing that had finally worn me down and impelled me to drag my family all the way to the bottom of the world was also having to deal with what *black* people thought they knew about me.

An illustration: When I first went to the *Washington Post,* I covered city government. One afternoon I was sitting at my desk in the press room of the District Building, Washington's city hall, when the mayor dropped by to banter with the press.

"Anybody home?" called Marion Barry.

This was the pre-cocaine-bust Marion Barry, when he still had a message and a mission—and still managed to get through the day reasonably sober. He was full of energy and anger and even genuine idealism, and I admired him in many ways. But he was an official and I was a reporter, and so we were natural enemies.

"What you doin' here, Mr. Mayor?" snapped Mike Davis, one of my competitors. Mike was a sharp-eyed veteran who had cut his teeth covering civil rights in the 1960s.

"You got nothing better to do with your time?" Mike asked the mayor. "Is this what the citizens of the District of Columbia are paying you for? Or are you just here for some pointers?"

"Pointers on what? What you got to teach me, Mike Davis?"

"Nothing, Mr. Mayor, 'cause you wouldn't listen. That's why you got no money in your pocket. Let me see, Mr. Mayor, what you got?"

Barry grinned, pulled a money clip out of his pocket and started counting out twenties. Mike pulled out *his* clip and started counting out *his* twenties. They both cheated—double-counting bills, inflating denominations—so the contest was inconclusive. It ended with the mayor and his aides and all the assembled reporters sharing a moment of laughter.

The mayor wheeled. "And what about you, Gene Robinson?"

My turn. But I had no clip full of twenties. And anyhow, for me there was no street-corner bonhomie. With me, the mayor was all leverage, all pressure, all business.

"When's your newspaper going to stop with all those bullshit stories?" he demanded. "Always negative. Always putting everything down, putting everybody down. Tearing down what little black leadership we have in this city. When are you going to wake up and start doing something positive for the people of Washington?"

"I do, Mr. Mayor," I said. "I write the truth."

He snorted. "The truth? What the hell does the *Washington Post* know about the truth? Whose truth? Not mine. Not the black people of this city's. Why don't you print *our* truth for a change, Gene Robinson?"

The mayor left, the entourage left, everyone went back to work, and I felt like slamming the wall. I felt like my rival Mike had won, the mayor had won, and I had clearly lost.

At that time I'd only been in Washington a few months. But here, in this bastion of the black middle class, here in Chocolate City, for the first time in my life it seemed that somehow I wasn't black enough. Perhaps more accurately, that I didn't quite know *how* to be black.

This was absurd and insulting on its face—I had grown up in the South and lived through the bitter end of segregation. But it was also true that I had spent my early years in a fairly unusual all-black environment, sheltered from anything resembling the accepted notion of the Urban Black Experience. I hadn't grown up in a ghetto. My mother wasn't a single parent, and life wasn't particularly tough. The streets weren't mean.

I hadn't gone to a historically black college, like Howard or Morehouse; instead, I'd gone off to the University of Michigan, where most of my good friends had been white. Afterward, I hadn't gone to New York or Washington or Detroit or Philadelphia, cities with long-established black communities and power structures that were bidding for control; I'd found my first job in San Francisco, viewed at the time as a weird place full of Asians and Hispanics as well as blacks, where the racial fault lines were harder to map than the many dangerous offshoots of the San Andreas. I'd married a black woman, but one who had been raised Catholic, attended an exclusive private high school, and developed her own distinctive way of navigating through the white world. I'm a confident person by nature, but suddenly I found myself actually wondering if I hadn't missed something somewhere along the way.

And there was more. It seemed that being black was supposed to mean sharing a certain set of attitudes, thinking in a certain way. Being almost paranoid. *White people were trying to take back the little power we had. White people wanted to deny us everything. White people were determined to tear our leaders down. White people this, white people that, white people, white people . . .*

My *Post* colleague Richard Cohen once reminded me that the word "paranoid" has no meaning for blacks and Jews, given what we've been through. But paranoia is also an abdication. To always imagine oneself a victim is to step aside, leaving center stage — and the capacity to act — to the protagonist, who happens to be the victimizer. He wins, you lose. It seemed to me that this was precisely what black people in Washington were doing, and that the logic that led to this abdication began with the traditional black-white zero sum view of race in America. It was a trap, a hole, and we were digging it ourselves.

I remember going to a community forum at a junior high school in the isolated part of Washington east of the marshy Anacostia River, far from the marble and the monuments and the Mall. It was the poorest and most crime-ridden part of the city, but the school was in a middle-class pocket, and that evening it was filled with civic-minded men and women determined not to let their neighborhood slip another inch down the slope. The occasion was the grilling of a panel of school board candidates. One of them, an ineffective incumbent, was taking more heat than she'd expected. She was dodging, weaving, sweating—but then she spotted me in the audience and launched into what by then was a familiar gambit.

Good things are happening in the schools, she said, but the press doesn't want you to know. They won't tell you the good things our elected officials and our schoolchildren are doing. Why is that? Why do you think that might be? We should ask the *Washington Post*. In fact, there was a young man from the *Washington Post* right over there, in the back row. Why not ask him?

People applauded, as I knew they would, and then turned in their chairs and craned their necks, searching out the interloper. I sat there attempting to look neutrally pleasant, or at least not evil, having been caught red-handed with notebook and pen.

That time, fortunately, I wasn't compelled to stand up and address the audience, as had sometimes happened. The discussion quickly got back to more pertinent questions, such as why test scores continued to fall and how it could be that books were in such short supply.

But afterward, it took me a half hour to get out of the hall. People were lined up to harangue me, to beseech me, to jab their fingers at my chest or gently take my arm and demand that I write the truth "for a change!"

When I got home, I needed a stiff drink.

Being black or white was not just physical, it was political. It was less a matter of race than racial identification. And, most important, it involved choosing sides.

Well, I was tired of choosing. I was tired of feeling under such constant scrutiny, sorted and categorized by whites, judged and sentenced by blacks. The whole idea of racial identification being the defining factor in one's life seemed wrong to me, oppressive and wrong, and there had to be a better way. I was fed up with the assumptions that white people made, fed up with the assumptions that black people made, fed up with suspicion and paranoia and seeing the world as us on the one side and them on the other. I was fed up enough with America to just pack up the family and leave.

So that's what I did. And that's how I ended up on that beach in Rio, where now I was learning that the limits established by those portraits on my living room wall back in Orangeburg were not absolute, that all of the labeling and the conflict and the angst that I had assumed came inevitably with the issue of race in America were, in fact, *optional.*

I KEEP COMING back to Rio and the beach because it was there that I first really understood that there were other ways to look at race than the way I was accustomed to seeing it, and that some of these ways might involve definitions of race radically different from my own.

American society sees race but not color; Brazilian society sees color but not race. It didn't take me long to figure out that this was an important distinction. What took much longer was to discover that the distinction wasn't quite as simple as it first seemed.

The emphasis on the more mutable issue of color (rather than the rigidity of race) was at the heart of what I loved so much about Brazil—the absence of racial conflict, the ease of coexistence. This was a big part of what made it feel so natural to me, so comfortable, to walk down the street or sit on the beach or mingle with a crowd in any part of the country. I could relax. There was no silent struggle going on.

But I could see that there was discrimination going on, beginning with discrimination in the sense of the word that means making fine distinctions. There were literally dozens of terms for skin color in Brazil—black, white, mulatto, and *pardo*, of course, but also more fanciful and evocative terms. In surveys, Brazilians have described themselves or others as "burned," "burned by the sun," "around midnight," "after midnight," "chocolate," "coffee with milk," and "navy blue." One particularly subtle and elusive hue was called "miscegenation." Brazilians I talked to would sometimes use these distinctions as simple descriptive tools, the way I might say a person was tall or short, thin or heavyset. It was jarring for me to hear people's skin color discussed in this way, but over time the impact lessened until it began to seem a normal topic of conversation.

There was another clear difference, one that made the two societies in a sense mirror images. American orthodoxy is that a single drop of African blood inevitably darkens its host. In Brazil, the problem is approached from the other end of the scale: A single drop of European blood is seen to inevitably whiten.

There is at least one clear, indisputable effect of the one-drop-darkens view of the world versus the every-little-bit-lightens view: The American scheme tends to maximize the number of black people, or people of color, or nonwhites—whatever term you prefer—within a given population, while the Brazilian view tends to minimize the count.

In the United States, if your father is black and your mother is white, then you're black—there is no way that our society is ready to consider the son of a black man anything but black. In Brazil, it's not that simple. If your father is white and your mother is black, then your own category will depend on a lot of things, most important your skin color. If you're very, very dark or very, very light, then it's an easy call. If you fall into a middling café au lait range of skin tones, then you're probably going to be thought of as more white than black.

Another effect, perhaps less clear-cut, involves the general level of racial tension. In Brazil, I learned, a person with discernible African heritage is not necessarily immutably black. If you're light-skinned, and if your hair can be called wavy instead of kinky, and if you're upwardly mobile, you can call yourself mulatto if you choose and perhaps even white. In the United States, black people can educate themselves and make money and enter the upper reaches of society, and still they and their children and their children's children will always be black. Except for a handful of people who "passed" as white, there has never been any conceivable way out, never been a means of escape. Black people thus had to make a stand. They had to demand their due from society as *black* people, now and forever. This led inevitably to ugly confrontation on a grand scale, and to more or less constant friction in the workplace and neighborhood.

It was a friction that I didn't notice until I'd been to a place where I could note its absence. Once or twice a year while we were overseas, we'd come back to the Washington area to visit; Avis's family lived in the Maryland suburbs, where she'd grown up. I'd invariably drop by the *Post*'s newsroom to say hello to my bosses and catch up with friends. And I'd leave, a couple of hours later, shaking my head and muttering under my breath and wishing I could catch the next plane.

I was always struck, on those visits, by the degree to which racial tension and overt conflict was an element of daily life. I'd ask friends how things were around the office, and the answer always seemed to have a racial subtext. Either "senior" reporters (which meant white reporters) were unhappy about being passed over, or black reporters were displeased with the rate of their progress, or whatever. Whether there was true conflict or not, whether there was even a real point of dispute or not, everything seemed to demand consideration in black and white.

My heart always sank. This was just what I had run away from. This was what had been strangling me.

I remember one time in particular when I asked a black colleague what had been happening since my last visit. He responded with a tour d'horizon of office politics in which every issue—who was going to cover city hall, how the city editor was treating her reporters, why the metro editor was displeased with his deputies—had something to do with race. I think if I had asked about the weather I would have gotten a recounting of the different ways in which blacks and whites were affected by the unusually warm summer.

I finally just tuned him out. "Is everybody here just stuck?" I asked Avis in frustration later. "Is everybody so stuck on race that they can't talk about anything else? Haven't we gotten anywhere?"

I'd asked my friend a question that called for either an individual response ("I'm fine") or a universal response ("Things are fine"), and instead I'd gotten a response based on group—specifically, based on racial group. More specific, I'd gotten this response from a man who had light-brown skin and wavy hair. A man who in the newsrooms of Rio de Janeiro would have had a hard time convincing people that he was black at all.

I WAS A BIT confused by what I'd seen in Brazil, a bit unmoored, but mostly I felt unencumbered—even liberated, to press an overused word into service. It was as if I had lived all my life next to a great wall, an insurmountable wall, resigned to the fact that no one could ever hope to get over it, and then one day I'd gone up in an airplane and discovered that others, not far away, dealt with the same wall by simply walking around it.

When we speak of race in America, we speak in the terminology of color—we say black and white and yellow and red and brown—but we don't really *mean* color at all, not the way they mean color in Brazil. What we really mean is racial identification, in the sense of group identification. We mean people who share a history, who share a culture, who share a status in the society, who even by and large share a political point of view—people who are assumed to share these things, I mean, even if reality doesn't bear these generalizations out. We associate the word "black" with speech patterns, taste in clothing, sense of humor, attributes that would seem to have little to do with skin color. We see race as something absolute and immutable, and we recognize no in-between; we've traditionally considered being "a little bit black" as impossible as being "a little bit pregnant."

Only in the past few years have Americans in any significant numbers begun to see this whole construct as wrong. From the affirmative action wars to the clamor for a new mixed-race category in the census, there have been calls—some disingenuous, to be sure, but others sincere and heartfelt—to jettison all the ballast we attach to race and see people as the individuals they are, nothing more and nothing less. To me, it amounted to an attempt to reshape the world into something new, something better.

In Brazil, I found that new world already built, furnished, and fully operational. Here was a place where people didn't just talk about an idealized rainbow society, they lived it. All around me, all the time, were people of every hue, every color of eye and texture of hair, every variant of cheekbone and hipbone, every width of nose and shape of chin, every curvature of breast and butt, mixed up in all possible combinations. Here was a place where someone like me, accustomed to a frame of reference where black was black and white was white, didn't even know where to begin drawing racial lines, let alone enforcing them. Here was a place where a kind of benign racial anarchy seemed to rule, a lubricious, frictionless chaos into which one could simply disappear.

I loved it, I reveled in it, I wallowed in it. It was just what I'd envisioned in my dreams, just the kind of freedom I'd always wanted. It wasn't until much later that I learned an old truth. In these matters of racial identity, as in so much else, the adage holds: We should be careful what we wish for, lest our wishes be granted.

Chapter 2

Behold the Promised Land

MY CURIOSITY ABOUT RACE IN BRAZIL, ON THAT FIRST TRIP OF many, grew out of my suspicion when I first arrived that somehow my plane had vectored off course and touched down in the Colored People's Promised Land.

Here I was in Rio de Janeiro, the urban jewel of a vast and populous nation, strolling the postcard-perfect beaches, gazing up at the modern skyscrapers, marveling at the upthrusting hills and verdant hanging valleys of one of the most beautiful cities in the world, and most of the people I saw around me in this paradise were black. They were black, at least, in my frame of reference, black in the American sense of having at least one visible drop of African blood.

There was no shortage of people I'd have classified as white, but they seemed a distinct minority. The acid test, for me, was that most of the people I saw would have looked seriously out of place at an American country club. To the extent that the identity of a nation is equivalent to the identity of its people, then Brazil was by my lights a great black nation—unadvertised as such, but a black nation nonetheless.

The man who officiously stamped my passport at the airport was black, as was the man who wheeled my suitcase to the curb while surreptitiously offering to change money at double the official rate, the man who tossed my things into the trunk of his cab and rocketed over hills and through tunnels as if on the circuit at Le Mans, the woman who took an impression of my credit card at the hotel reception desk. A black woman sold me a city map at the hotel gift shop; a black man standing behind the hotel bar mixed me one of those ambrosial firewater-and-lime concoctions called a *caipirinha*. It was a narrow, unrepresentative slice of the country that I saw those first few hours, but I was smitten. This was a huge, impressive place, a world-class place, and so many of the people here, or at least the ones I'd seen, were people of color. Having read for so many years about all the various basket-case nations of Africa, I thought I saw in Brazil an absolute revelation—and a source of some considerable pride.

As soon as I could, I brought the family to Rio, marvelous Rio, the city I'd come to love so much and was dying to share. Rio was my Paris. I knew Avis would just love Rio.

She hated it.

Actually, that's not quite true: She didn't really hate Rio, she just liked the other places she'd seen in Brazil better. She found Rio crowded, smelly, tourist-slick, and overly intent upon separating us from our hard-earned money. All of which was true, and, I felt, somewhat beside the point.

"Isn't that beautiful?" I kept saying.

"Ugh. What's that smell?" she kept saying.

But there was a weak point in that armor. Avis had been an accomplished dancer in high school and college. There was simply no way that she could help but feel the city's constant rhythm. True to form, it only took a day or so for the spirit to grab her: She announced that she wanted to go dancing, and not at one of those tourist-trap floor-show joints. It had to be authentic. The hotel arranged a baby-sitter for Aaron, who was then just five years old, and a driver cum guide for us, and late one Friday night we set out to samba.

There are a dozen and a half major "samba schools" in Rio, really not schools at all, but neighborhood associations of a sort, existing primarily to compete against one another each year in the grand, glittering *carnaval* parade. The final competition is held over two days in a huge grandstand downtown called the Sambadrome. There's nothing comparable in the United States, although the Mardi Gras "krewes" in New Orleans would probably be closest. The "schools" spend the whole year planning for *carnaval*, choosing a theme, designing floats and costumes, writing the words and music for a special *carnaval* samba, and most of all practicing the ordered chaos of the grand parade. Five thousand or more people march for each school in the competition, the multitudes divided into "wings" that have different costumes and different roles to play in what amounts to an allegorical pageant. In recent years, the *carnaval* themes have tended toward sex—one year, a group used the theme "Everybody Was Born Naked" and proceeded to demonstrate how to revert to that original state of grace—and toward history, especially the history of Brazilian slavery and the continuation of the nation's African heritage. *Carnaval*, after all, had started as a black celebration. The word "spectacular" doesn't begin to do it justice.

It is truly the greatest show on earth, and one of the reasons why is that it takes so much time and effort to prepare.

And so much money. To raise the necessary funds, the samba schools advertised their practice sessions and charged admission. And so, with *carnaval* just a couple of months away, Avis and I found ourselves being driven far from the beaches and the tourist hotels, through industrial zones and forbidding slums, looking for the auditorium of a samba school called Salgueiro.

The place announced its presence with noise—cars, crowds, honking, shouting, a thudding samba beat that was more felt than heard. We parked, and the driver led us through steel doors into a warehouse-sized space full of light, color, movement, sound. At least a couple of thousand members and fans of Salgueiro, many dressed in the Salgueiro colors, red and white, were packed onto a vast dance floor.

Part of the band—the singers, guitarists, and horn players— occupied a long stage, belting and strumming and blowing the year's chosen samba over and over again, the repetition designed to imbed it in the brain so that by the time the big day came every-one would know it not just by heart but by bone, sinew, and soul as well. "*Vai, tristeza!*" they yelled. "Away, sadness!" Every school's samba, it seemed, wanted to banish unhappiness in some way or another. The rest of the band, the drum corps, was pounding away in a balcony high above the entrance, up where the walls and ceil-ing were decorated with brightly colored *Miami Vice* neon.

Our driver led us through the crowd and I was enchanted, not just with the intoxicating music and movement but also with the crowd itself. It was dizzyingly, even breathtakingly multicolored.

I know that sounds like an odd or even ridiculous thing to no-tice in the midst of so much visual and aural stimulation, but there you have it: Like most black people in America, I'd grown up with race a constant presence in my consciousness, a permanent element in my field of vision, a nagging pressure. To walk into a huge crowd and suddenly have the sensation that race didn't even exist was disorienting, a natural high.

There were black people and white people and brown people and all manner of people, and they followed no familiar pattern. They were all mixed up, blacks with whites, dark browns with light browns, in constant motion. It wasn't like an interracial crowd in America, where there would have been clumps of white folks and black folks, where some group would have predominated, where some people would have looked comfortable and at home and some others less comfortable and less at home. Here there was no sense of that kind of division. There was plenty of electricity in the air—musical, celebrational, especially sexual— but one familiar kind was missing. There was no racial electricity in this multiracial crowd. I'm sure that some people wouldn't even have noticed, but my attention was riveted by this conspicuous absence.

I didn't fully trust my senses, and yet I knew what I was seeing was more than an illusion. Something was fundamentally different here, despite all the things that were superficially the same.

Our driver took us upstairs, to a spectators' gallery, where he introduced us to a man he called the *chefao*, the big boss. He was thin and tan-skinned, wearing a bright red suit, a white silk shirt open at the neck, and lots of gold; his handshake was weak, his stare cold and hard, almost reptilian. He went by the name Miro; I later found out that he was one of the biggest numbers-game tycoons in Rio, and the chief patron of Salgueiro. Gangsters ran *carnaval*, and ran it pretty well.

The rest of the evening is pretty much a blur. We danced, we drank, we went to another samba school, Vila Isabel, where we danced some more. We got home at about three or four. But I've never forgotten the look and feel and impact of that crowd at Salgueiro.

It is difficult to describe the absence of something, and yet it is that absence that was so striking. I believe that that was the first time in my life that I'd been in a multiracial crowd and sensed no racial walls between people. In part, this was due to my own ignorance; in such a crowd in America, I'd have been able to look at people and pick up reliable clues about income and status and the like and then, armed with these assumptions, I could have imagined the walls into being. If I were at a pro basketball game in Washington, for example, and saw a middle-aged white guy in Dockers and penny loafers standing next to a young black guy in baggy jeans and a bright yellow windbreaker, then I'd automatically—and subconsciously—erect a wall. I didn't know those signals well enough in Brazil. But there was more to it than my inexperience. There was an ease with which people interacted, an intimacy, a complicity. There was an absence of discomfort among dark people and light people. It was as if I'd discovered a new world, a new way to be.

I'd found Another Way—a way for people to deal with one another without all the tension and friction and anger that I felt in America. I'd found a system that let people be themselves, that let people be individuals, rather than exemplars of groups.

I had a new way of looking at the world, and I never, ever, wanted to go back to the old way.

That interlude in Rio came at the end of a long trip we took through Brazil as a family, Avis, Aaron, and I, one of the few times we all got to travel together. This whole South America thing was an adventure and, in many ways, a scary one. We were a long, long way from friends and family, entirely on our own, and all we really had was one another. The trip helped cement the bonds among us, gave us new confidence in our little family's ability to chew this great big mouthful we'd just bitten off.

I also thought of it as a deposit in the "family togetherness" bank, against which I would later draw—make that wildly overdraw—with my constant traveling.

We spent a few days in Salvador, the old capital and slave port, with its remarkable colonial architecture and its spicy fattening food. Our hotel was on the beach, and so, practically as soon as we arrived, we went out to frolic in the sand and the waves. By then I was accustomed to the usual sights on any Brazilian beach—the palm trees, the coconut vendors, the perfect brown bodies in the tiniest swimsuits imaginable—but for Avis, it was a new experience.

She surveyed the scene with a skeptical eye, first looking out at the bronzed and toned multitudes, and then considering her own swimwear, a one-piece suit that would have been slightly daring at Hilton Head or the Outer Banks.

"I've got a problem," she said to me.

"Problem?"

"Problem. I feel like I'm wearing an overcoat."

The salesclerk at the hotel gift shop, a brown-skinned, heavyset woman with a pretty face and green eyes, helped her pick out a more appropriate swimsuit, one consisting of mere square centimeters of fabric. String bikinis and skimpy one-pieces in Brazil are referred to as *fio dental*—dental floss. Avis tried it on and gave me an even more skeptical look.

"You have a beautiful body," the saleswoman coaxed. "You can't hide it, not here. This is Brazil." So Avis did the Brazilian thing—she bought it and wore it.

In Salvador's graceful old colonial quarter, we took a wonderful photograph of Aaron chasing a flock of pigeons across a plaza ringed by graceful old churches. He loved watching the street performers practice *capoeira,* a unique Brazilian martial art that's part dance, part tae kwan do, and he loved the mournful sound of the *berimbau,* a single-stringed instrument that's like an archer's bow with a gourd at one end that provided the soundtrack for the *capoeira* street theater. He liked it so much, in fact, that we had to buy him one.

We were stranded unexpectedly during what was supposed to be a one-hour stopover in Belém, a graceful old dowager of a city at the mouth of the Amazon. "The plane," our pilot explained helpfully, "is broken." It took two days for the necessary replacement part to arrive; the airline officials lodged us and our fellow travelers in a nice hotel and then amused themselves by giving the stingiest, most cryptic progress reports imaginable on the progress of the repairs and our prospects for ever being able to leave.

So we explored. We strolled past the rotting old market down by the wharf, where buzzards wheeled and perched and lifted and wheeled again by the thousands. We walked through the old residential quarters, past houses with wrought-iron gates and stone walls that were slick and greenish with lichen. From street vendors we sampled ice creams with bright, alien, tropical flavors, made from rain forest fruits we'd never heard of and couldn't begin to pronounce. This wasn't Ben and Jerry's; this was Brazil.

Finally we just took a cab to the airport and made noise until they found us a plane that would take us to our next scheduled stop: Manaus, the famed Amazon metropolis built during the nineteenth-century rubber boom.

From the city limits of Manaus, in any direction you choose, there's nothing but hundreds of miles of the thickest rain forest left on earth. Our hotel had a little private zoo whose menagerie included a jaguar and a boa constrictor—not, thankfully, a petting zoo. We took a cruise on the impossibly wide rivers, chugging out to the point where the wine-dark waters of the Río Negro meet the milky brown waters of the Amazon in giant lingering fractal swirls. On a river island we saw lily pads three feet in diameter. As part of the standard excursion, the economic development part, we were also taken to visit a pitiful little Indian village; there, the men and women and children sullenly did themselves up daily in sad feathers and haphazard face paint and sold crafts to the tourists. It was heartbreaking and depressing to see proud people reduced to such a joyless pantomime.

But at this point in our jourey, the news saw fit to intervene.

I left Avis and Aaron in Manaus for a couple of days while I flew off to the far western Amazon to cover a flare-up in the violent conflict between rubber tappers and cattle ranchers. The precipitating event was the arrest of a couple of suspects in the murder of a noted ecologist and union activist named Chico Mendes; he had been organizing the rubber tappers and the local ranchers hated him to the point of wanting him dead. The suspects, a father-son duo who owned a sizable ranch, had just been nabbed in a dusty little riverbend town called Rio Branco. I figured that since I was in the neighborhood I'd check the story out.

This side trip was an impulsive decision, and the instant I arrived at the Rio Branco airport I regretted it. Here I was, in the middle of the Amazon, much closer to the Pacific Ocean than I was to Rio or São Paulo, not knowing a soul, armed only with the name of a hotel plucked from a travel guide and a paltry vocabulary in Portuguese that barely got me a taxi ride into town. I dropped my things in the hotel room, went outside, walked twice around the tree-lined central plaza, went back inside, came out again into the plaza, and finally sat down on a bench to try to figure out where to start.

Across the square I noticed a big building labeled POLICIA MILITAR. For lack of a better idea, I marched through the entrance, into a big courtyard, and started looking for somebody to talk to. I blundered into an office where a few men, whom I took to be plainclothes policemen, were sitting around shooting the breeze. One of them, the man in charge, came up to greet me: Sergeant Jairo Texeira de Sousa, at my service, and wondering what the hell I was doing there. He had a gun strapped into a shoulder holster and a decidedly steely gaze, but something about him put me more at ease than I had any objective right to be, his manner, his tone, and not least the fact that he was a black man.

"Americano?" he said, hearing my fractured attempt at Portuguese. Then in Spanish: "You like Stevie Wonder?"

Jairo, who had wavy hair and a reddish cast that indicated some Indian blood, spoke enough Spanish for the two of us to communicate. He announced that we were brothers, and then spent the next two days squiring me around town, introducing me to the environmentalists, the ranchers, the local authorities — even to the two murder suspects themselves, who were languishing in a prison on the outskirts of town. This penal facility consisted of a dilapidated set of low-slung buildings set around weed-choked open spaces. For some reason there were white, humpbacked zebu cattle roaming freely through the grounds. The suspects, for the record, said they didn't do it. Just before Jairo and I were about to leave to go back to town, the skies opened up in a tropical downpour, the heaviest I'd ever seen, sheets of rain that came slamming and crashing down in a terrible racket—and then suddenly stopped, leaving nothing but silence and steam.

Jairo had taken good care of me, had proved to be an able "fixer." I knew enough about the Third World to realize that, at the end of all this, I should offer him a tip of some kind. I also had a sense of how paltry the salaries of federal military policemen were. So before I left for the airport, I discreetly offered him a couple of twenties.

He refused to accept them.

"Friends," he said, and that was that.

The result was a good story, but, more important, a deepening of my infatuation with Brazil. Even in the middle of the jungle, hundreds of miles from nowhere, there were people of color, people with whom I felt an instant affinity, and who reciprocated. Even in the darkest Amazon, I was never alone.

The whole trip was like that. Everywhere, there were colored people: the crowds in the streets in all the cities; the cartwheeling *capoeira* dancers in Salvador who'd entranced Aaron with their spins and their kicks; the dental-floss saleswoman at the hotel gift shop; the ice cream vendors in Belém with their unpronounceable treats; the skipper in Manaus who took us out to see the meeting of the waters.

This was Brazil. Everywhere, there was color; and everywhere, we felt as comfortable as could be. This was a tonic, because the three of us were all a bit ultrasensitive to race, having felt especially conspicuous in our new home in Buenos Aires.

We loved most aspects of B.A., but there was no escaping the fact that the Argentine people were obviously, and in some ways insistently, white. It was a society of European immigrants with something of an inferiority complex regarding the old countries of Italy and Spain. In the 1920s and 1930s Argentina had been one of the six or seven most developed nations on earth; since then it had slid and racheted and tumbled steadily downhill, and the haughty Argentines had a complex about that, too. They weren't rich anymore, and they weren't truly European. But at least they were white.

One time in the Miami airport, waiting to catch a plane to Buenos Aires, I was at once charmed and repelled by an elderly Argentine woman who regaled me in her perfect English with tales of the city's glory days, but who then, without a hint of self-consciousness, began a harangue about how offended she was at the suggestion, made by a U.S. customs officer, that she mark "Hispanic" on her entry form. That she would raise such a topic to me, a black American, seemed simply bizarre, but I finally decided that it simply hadn't occurred to her that anyone would take offense.

"Why, we are white!" she said, clearly exercised. "Anyone can see that!"

And so, by and large, they were. In Buenos Aires, a city of ten million people, there were so few black people that Avis, Aaron, and I stuck out like sore thumbs. Passersby would stare at us in the street; children would point and giggle.

Avis, with her close-cropped hair and flashing eyes, was for the Argentines some kind of exotic Jezebel, sexy beyond measure. A lot of people mistook her to be Brazilian. Aaron, to his great discomfort, was a totem: Some old superstition indicated that it was good luck to rub a black child's head, and since he was the only black child that any given passerby was likely to see on any given day, people would go to great lengths to come near enough for a quick swipe.

As for me, they looked at a tall black man and thought one thing: basketball. The only tall black men most Argentines were likely to have seen on the street were Americans who had come south to play basketball in the Argentine professional league. People would approach me four or five times a day and make a little motion with their hands, which I finally figured out was meant to imitate dribbling a basketball. "*Jugás al basquet?*" they'd ask. At first, I politely told them no; then, as I became more and more annoyed, my answers got more brusque. I never lied and said yes, even though I was tempted at times. I just didn't want to reinforce the stereotype that any tall black American man had to be a basketball player.

Within a few days of landing in B.A., we'd all learned what it must have felt like to live in one of those new-style kind-to-the-animals free-range zoos—unconfined, perhaps, but never un-watched.

After a few months of this, coming to Brazil and suddenly being among people who looked so much like us was an enormous relief. My trips to Rio were so exhilarating, in fact, that I became fixated on the idea of blending in: Here was a place where I could walk down the street and pass as a native, where I wouldn't have to feel as if I were on stage all the time. Here nobody would stare.

I was childishly disappointed when I went out for the first time to stroll along Copacabana Beach, and the trinket sellers and con artists and shills all swarmed to me like bees to walking honey, buzzing around in their hard-won phrasebook English. The skin might be right, I finally realized, but everything else was wrong: I was dressed like an American, with big, baggy swimming trunks and Docksider-type boat shoes.

Retreating to the hotel shop, I bought one of these little pouch-style bathing suits that Brazilian men wear, along with a pair of standard-issue rubber sandals, and went back out. The swarm returned. This time, it took a while to figure out why: I was wearing a wristwatch and my big gold wedding band, and no *carioca* (as Rio residents call themselves) in his right mind would ever dream of wearing a single piece of jewelry to the beach, for fear of being robbed.

More determined than ever, I went back to the hotel, stashed the watch and ring in the room safe, and tried again. I kept at it until finally I could walk down the street unmolested. When I clumsily bumped into a man carrying armfuls of "I ♥ Rio" T-shirts, and instead of trying to sell me one he cursed me passionately and lengthily in Portuguese, I knew I'd arrived.

This wasn't something I necessarily could have pulled off quite so easily in Lagos, say, or Accra. My personal gene pool is overwhelmingly African, but not purely so; there's a splash of European and at least a dollop of Native American somewhere in the murky depths. In Brazil, with its history of African slavery and Indian conquest—a history so much like our own—there would be thousands of people, almost certainly many thousands, whose ethnicity was made from precisely the same recipe as mine, with the same ingredients in just the same proportions. My mirror image, my ethnic double, my long-lost twin doubtless could be found somewhere here on the same crowded beach I was walking. Here was another place in the world, thousands of miles from home, where if I worked hard enough at it I could blend in completely—where I could belong.

It's a cliché to point out that we African Americans don't have an "old country" to belong to. We have an old continent— and a vaguely defined and distant one at that—a place whose history, by and large, is obscure and incomplete, and whose peoples claim primary allegiance to ethnic groups, tribes, and clans that mean the world to them and nothing at all to us. We're so far removed physically and psychologically from Africa that the continent itself is more a pleasant daydream than anything else, a source of a possible identity that we can no longer confirm. I knew many black Americans who had come to know Africa and ended up loving it—and a few who'd ended up hating it, or at least rejecting it—but none who'd felt they truly belonged. None who believed, even after spending years in Africa, that they ever *could* belong.

After only five minutes in Brazil, I knew instinctively that belonging was not only possible, but somehow already half-accomplished. I felt oddly at home.

The people I saw around me in Rio de Janeiro were of such infinite variety that no one I could think of ever having met was automatically excluded, strictly on the basis of coloring or features, from being Brazilian, just as no one in the world can be definitively ruled out as a possible American. But there were some expatriates I met in Brazil who, through a combination of ethnicity and attitude, screamed to all the world that they manifestly did not belong, and never would.

An Austrian journalist named Hans, who had an apartment not far from Copacabana, had been living and working in Rio about a year, and somehow managed to get mugged, on average, about once every three months. He was slight, blond, hopelessly Aryan, and notoriously bad with the language, and on top of it all he announced with a more or less permanent sneer that he didn't really want to be here. He felt, as did Charles de Gaulle, that Brazil was "not a serious country." Brazil seemed to have sensed this disdain, and to have responded in kind. Muggers ignored little old ladies with gold necklaces draping their wattled necks and wads of money spilling out of their purses in order to go straight for Hans. The muggings were getting rougher, too, from muscle to knifepoint to gunpoint; meanwhile, Hans hardened his attitude and widened his sneer, creating a kind of feedback loop. We all thought he should leave, and leave soon, before he got himself shot.

By contrast, my good friend Mac Margolis blended into the country so seamlessly that many people who met him for the first time took him for a native. Mac, a journalist and author, had abandoned his New England roots to come south and ended up falling in love with Brazil. A planned sojourn of a couple of years had stretched into an indefinite stay—competence in Portuguese had turned into total fluency, and he'd become something of a fixture in Rio. For a while I jokingly called him "Amazon Mac" because he'd spent a lot of time out there and become a real expert; later he turned that expertise into quite a good book, called *The Last New World*.

Mac worked out of a hillside house, perched tenuously on Sugarloaf's low shoulder, that had been converted into office suites and an all-purpose hangout for the city's expatriate journalists: the unfortunate Hans; a manqué British aristocrat named Ivo Dawnay, one of a succession of correspondents from the *Financial Times* of London; Bill Long, a consummate professional from the *Los Angeles Times*; assorted freelancers, television producers, radio reporters, and hangers-on.

Mac's workspace consisted of the penthouse. From his terrace he enjoyed one of Rio's signature views, with the sweep of Botafogo Bay set against the city's skyline, and in the background a ridge of tall, green mountains climbing in steps to Corcovado, the greenest and tallest of all, topped by the famous statue of Christ the Redeemer with his arms outstretched to embrace a world of deadly sin and incomparable beauty. I'd go to Mac's office to use his files and get some work done, with nothing but good intentions of arranging interviews and polishing off stories, and instead I'd end up doing nothing but standing on the terrace and staring at that amazing view.

With his dark hair and coloring Mac almost looked mulatto, which he wasn't. But he carried himself like a Brazilian; he'd lived in Rio long enough that all his clothing was Brazilian, and nobody on the street would ever have thought to give him a second look.

Mac often contributed stories to the *Post,* so I saw him every time I came to town. Usually we'd walk down the steep, twisting, concrete stairs that led to the neighborhood below, with its tiny tourist-free beach, and have lunch at a little restaurant called Garota da Urca. Over passable food and tall bottles of ice-cold beer I'd interrogate him at length and in detail about the wonderful country he'd adopted.

"If you love Brazil, then it might love you back," he told me early on. "If you hate it, it knows."

He was preaching to the choir, though. And despite the fact that I wrote any number of stories about Brazil's horrible poverty and its vastly unfair income distribution and the endemic violent crime that amounted to undeclared class warfare—despite all that, I never had a bit of trouble in Brazil. No one ever tried to rob me, no one ever tried to take advantage of me, no one ever treated me with anything like contempt. I felt at ease, and because of that ease I felt a certain superiority over other outsiders who suffered—like Hans. In fact, I took their suffering not as proof of any deficiency on the part of Brazil or its people, even the people who made their living robbing others with knives and guns, but as evidence of some failure on the part of the sufferers. It was Hans's fault that he kept getting mugged. I was that gaga over the place.

I loved the fact that Brazil was a big, continent-sized country; as an American, I suppose I'm always most comfortable knowing

that the frontier lies several time zones away. I loved the pulsing
music I heard everywhere and the loping pace of life and the remarkable sense of individual style that everyone seemed to have.

Most of all, I loved the ease with which people of all colors
seemed to mix and mingle and match. Groups who arrived at the
beach together, or walked together down the street, were all
mixed up, with skin tones that covered the whole spectrum. I'd
often seen that sort of mixed group in an American big city downtown at lunchtime, because the American workplace has finally
become more or less integrated. I hadn't often seen it, though, on
an American beach on a weekend, or in an American park on the
Fourth of July. I was accustomed to seeing, instead, Americans
in color-coordinated clumps—brown ones here, pink ones there.
Here in Brazil, if I could trust the evidence of my eyes, was Martin Luther King's dream given substance and flesh, a place where
black, white, yellow, brown, and red were so mixed and matched
that the kind of racism I was used to in the United States seemed
simply not practicable. Wasn't this indeed the nonracial, essentially color-blind Promised Land?

"It's not that simple," Mac kept telling me. He urged me to
read a freelance article he'd written for the *Post* about race in
Brazil. It was subtle, nuanced, and somewhat negative in tone,
and, to my mind, unconvincing. I thought Mac was focusing on
the obscure and ignoring the obvious. I thought, frankly, that as a
white American, despite all his experience and all his facility with
the language, he just couldn't see the situation as clearly as a
black American. He was analyzing the country intellectually,
while I was feeling its presence. And I was in no mood for unnecessary complication.

After all, I was home.

Chapter 3

Cocoon

WHILE I WAS GROWING UP DURING THE FIFTIES AND THE SIXTIES, the rule in Orangeburg and throughout the rest of the South was racial segregation. It was more than a rule; it was the way things were.

Orangeburg had black neighborhoods and white neighborhoods, or rather a black side of town and a white side; there were black schools and white; there were of course black churches and white churches, as there are to this day. Separation was far from complete, since some blacks worked in the households of whites, or in their stores or their factories or their fields, as had been the case for hundreds of years. In that sense, there was a measure of intimacy between the races, although it's arguable whether such an unequal relationship can be truly intimate. Commerce also brought blacks and whites together, since blacks represented about half the city's population and almost half its purchasing power. White merchants—with a few die-hard, Johnny Reb exceptions—were happy to welcome paying black customers, though sometimes through a separate entrance.

I remember walking among white people when my mother took me to Fersner's five-and-dime, with its dark squeaking wooden floor and its permanent smell of popcorn, or to Phillips' Shoes, where I could ride the little merry-go-round in the rear part of the store while my mother looked at pair after pair of shoes in the front. Those two stores were downtown, on Russell Street, just down from the town square, with its Confederate memorial, and not far from the county jail, a pastel monstrosity that everyone called the Pink Palace. Also downtown was a movie theater, the only one in town. By the time I was old enough to go to movies, black people were allowed to sit anywhere they wanted, not just their traditional assigned perch in the balcony.

Although I saw white people every day, I didn't really know any. I'd had contact with white doctors—one delivered me, one took my tonsils out, one treated my colds and flus and bronchitis, one prescribed my first pair of eyeglasses when I was six—but it's fair to say that until I went to high school, my direct interpersonal experience with white people was practically nil.

This was partly due to the fact that the black half of Orangeburg was unusual, although I had no inkling of this at the time. The city is the home of two historically black schools, South Carolina State College and Claflin College. My mother, Louisa Smith Robinson, was head librarian at Claflin; my father, Harold I. Robinson, who has a law degree, taught political science there for a time. I grew up in a college town. Almost all my parents' friends had some connection with one or the other of the two schools, as professors, administrators, librarians, coaches, chaplains, former teachers, graduate students. Everyone, it seemed, had an advanced degree. In formal settings, lifelong friends would ostentatiously address one another as Dr. This and Dr. That to underscore the achievement the title represented. The boast, perhaps apocryphal, was that Orangeburg had more black Ph.D.'s per capita than any other city in the United States. Achievement was expected, and anything less was unacceptable.

Anything less, in fact, was worthy of contempt. My friend Jimmy Sherman's father, who taught at another black college in a town a few miles away, went out to the University of Oklahoma to get his doctorate. Commuting home during breaks, he completed the coursework; then he began work on his dissertation. But this sort of long-distance study was an ordeal, even more of an ordeal than writing a doctoral dissertation usually is, and it took him months and months, and then years and years. The reaction of his peers? People laughed at him cruelly behind his back. The man couldn't even finish his doctorate! In a clucking tone, usually reserved for deadbeats who'd abandoned their children, people would ask, "Why doesn't Sherman just *finish?*"

As a result of all this accomplishment and brain power and quiet arrogance, Orangeburg was probably more self-contained and self-sufficient than most black communities in the South, or, for that matter, most black communities in the sophisticated North. But it was a hard-won triumph; the black people of Orangeburg had to be resourceful, making what they could of an intolerable situation, in many cases turning deprivation into a kind of victory. It was a brutal time, a disgraceful era in which people were systematically denied basic human dignity because of their color, and routinely beaten or jailed or even shot for demanding it. Those advanced degrees that everyone had, for example, were earned at faraway universities like Michigan or Syracuse or Penn

State or Oklahoma, since the schools closer to home still hadn't
gotten around to admitting blacks. This meant that my friends'
parents, like Jimmy Sherman's father, sometimes would have to
leave their families for months at a time to pursue some course of
study in some frigid cow town a thousand miles away. My own
father commuted to work for a time all the way to Atlanta, then a
five- or six-hour drive, coming home only on weekends. This
kind of thing was an awful hardship, but it was also broadening,
exposing these voyagers to people and places and ideas they otherwise would have missed. I felt that the black people I knew
from church or the campuses were much more connected with
the wider world than were the residents of narrow, provincial
white Orangeburg just a few miles across town.

The truth is that we never envied white Orangeburg because
it just wasn't very interesting. It was a southern agricultural community, the commercial center for a fairly prosperous midstate
county planted with peanuts, soybeans, cotton, and corn. Orangeburg wasn't exactly isolated—it straddled U.S. 301, which
was one of the most important north-south corridors on the East
Coast before the interstates were built—but neither was it part of
any larger metropolis. The tallest building in town, the redbrick
Hotel Eutaw, was eight stories high. Besides South Carolina
State and Claflin, the city's only claim to even statewide fame was
the beauty of Edisto Gardens, a spectacularly manicured park
planted with roses and azaleas alongside the slow, dark Edisto
River, its banks lined with oaks and cypresses dangling long, gray
beards of Spanish moss. Beyond that there wasn't much to Orangeburg except converging rail lines and a big John Deere tractor dealership.

The accident of my upbringing led me to do to whites what
they have done to blacks for so many years—develop stereo-

types, based on evidence that was both anecdotal and arbitrary. White people, in my childhood experience, were farmers and merchants, with a few professionals thrown in. They were wealthier than black people, they lived in bigger houses, they drove nicer cars; they had power, and in many circumstances they were to be feared, in the sense that if you saw four white youths coming down the sidewalk toward you, the prudent thing to do was cross over, since they might think they had the right to start trouble and you knew that any trouble was likely to end worse for the blacks than for the whites. But in general, white people weren't very well educated; they drove pickup trucks, as far as I could see, and drank beer, and spent a lot of time hunting and fishing, but they didn't seem to have any intellectual ambition. They didn't seem to have any other kind of ambition either, at least not compared to the colored people I saw around me. Colored people wanted their children to grow and learn and leave Orangeburg and go to New York or Washington or Atlanta and make something of their lives. White people seemed to want their children to stay home and work in the family drugstore or sell auto parts. There were a few exceptions, of course, the white doctors and lawyers who wanted their pampered sons to grow up to be doctors and lawyers, too—and their pampered daughters to marry doctors or lawyers—but of these, there didn't seem to be many. The white people I saw as a child had extremely rough edges, showed little appreciation for culture, and were years behind the times in almost all regards. And they certainly didn't speak standard English very well.

I realize now, with perfect hindsight, that my coal-to-cream world was a small, relatively privileged slice of black Orangeburg. Most black people in town lived in neighborhoods like Sunnyside, down in the bottomland near the river, with its tin-roofed shacks of weathered wood perched on rickety stilts. They had no connection with the colleges and no advanced degrees; they were poor, poorly educated, and highly dependent on the crumbs that white Orangeburg occasionally saw fit to toss their way. My recalled impressions of Sunnyside are of barefoot children playing jump rope in clean but tattered clothes, the fabric so thin from washing that you could read through it; of dark, heavy women sitting in the heat on the decrepit porches, trying to stir up a breeze with cardboard paddle-fans from church, fans decorated with airbrushed portraits of a brown-haired, fair-skinned, blue-eyed Jesus; of thin, bent men worn down by the years, men in flapping old shoes and frayed old pants, men with bad teeth and often with the smell of cheap liquor on their breath. These people worked hard all their lives and paid their taxes and got nothing, nothing at all, in return.

The schools they got for their hard-earned money, for example, were awful. Whereas the white public schools were generally good, the black public schools were criminally underfunded and undersupplied. This I saw only from a distance, though, because there was never any thought of sending me or my younger sister, Ellen, to any of the public grade schools. There was a black Catholic school, Christ the King, that was pretty good, but we weren't Catholic, and so that was hardly an option for us either.

My sister and my friends and I all went to an institution that amounted to an all-black academy: Felton Training School, a laboratory school on the campus of South Carolina State that was the best school in town, black or white. It was a four-room schoolhouse where four formidable teachers—Mrs. Flossie Clinkscales, Mrs. Lovely Mae White, Mrs. Geneva Edwards, and Mrs. Alba Lewis—kept order in eight unruly grades, two grades to a room. Mrs. White, the darkest of the four, with skin the color of semisweet chocolate, used to keep order by threatening to "shake your liver loose." She never did, of course, but for two years I lived in mortal fear of having my internal organs rearranged.

My mother, who thankfully keeps everything, has kept a photograph of the whole Felton student body taken around 1961 when I would have been seven. Today I can go down the rows and pick out the kids who grew up to make grand successes of their lives: Belinda Davis, the lawyer; Chuck Disher, the Wall Street banker; Toni Whaley, the dentist; Jimmy Sherman, the air force colonel. Felton was a strivers' school, a place where current and future achievement was expected—not just expected, demanded—and where no excuses were acceptable.

So I was never tempted to confuse race with achievement, at least not in the way those two things are most commonly confused in this country. Nor did I confuse it with intelligence, or capacity, or drive. But I could hardly have missed the clear relationship between race and power: one's racial identity meant either having it or not.

It was a lesson that every black boy or girl quickly learned in the segregated South. I was bucktoothed and needed braces, so we found an orthodontist upstate in Florence, a city an hour and a half away—a white orthodontist. He always made us wait in his private office, rather than in the waiting room where we might have offended the bucktoothed white boys and girls and their parents. He was more than willing to take our money, though. So were the gas stations along the way, although more often than not they had three bathrooms—men, women, and colored. This was patently illegal by then, but who was going to do anything about it? There were many times when a truck full of beer-swilling white men would drive past our house, and they'd stare with a very specific kind of malevolence, one that seemed to stop just short of violence. It was all about power: they had it and we didn't.

Incidents like these stand out in my memory now like talismans or gemstones; there's something that feels hard-won about them, something that I want always to keep with me, never to forget. But the truth is that segregation and Jim Crow were such a part of the wallpaper of my everyday world, so like the earth and the sky and the trees, that I didn't even recognize many of their effects until much later, when as an adult I could look back, turn events over in my mind and see little anomalies, and then trace those anomalies back to race.

I have vivid recollections of the summer trips we'd take by car to visit my other grandmother, my father's mother, who lived in Michigan. We'd provision heavily, with enough food and drink, it seemed, for a nuclear evacuation. We'd have sandwiches, fried chicken, thermoses full of cold drinks, big slabs of pound cake, fruit, snacks. The car was often so full that there was barely room for me: I remember riding up above the backseat, on the ledge beneath the rear window. (Fortunately, Ellen was just a baby and could ride with my mother; otherwise, I don't know where my parents would have stowed me.) The stages of our trips were calibrated according to the rest stops where my father planned to pull off the road so we could stretch and eat. Maps were marked, distances ascertained, contingencies taken into account. Successful military campaigns make do with less planning and logistics.

I later learned that all prudent black families driving through the segregated South used to travel this way, not because we were really afraid the Russians were about to send their missiles or anything like that, but because we weren't going to be able to buy any food on the road. Many of those roadside diners we passed were whites-only and would have refused our business if we'd been naive or foolhardy enough to stop and ask.

We never stopped at any of the motels that advertised SWIMMING POOL or TV IN ROOM, instead pushing ahead through winding mountain roads until we reached Charleston, West Virginia, where we always went to the same hotel. It had small rooms and no pool and no television, and the beds were so close together they almost touched. I remember thinking that if this was what hotels were like, it was a wonder that anyone ever wanted to stay in one. But that was where we stayed, because it was a "colored" hotel, one of the few along our route. The others just wouldn't have us.

Whenever we'd get to Columbus, Ohio, we'd stop at the same city playground, an ordinary playground behind a chain-link fence, where I'd burn off some of my energy on the swings and the monkey bars and plunge down the biggest sliding board I'd ever seen. It was just a garden-variety playground, really nothing special about it, but to me it was the best playground in the world—because back home in Orangeburg, the well-equipped city playground was off-limits to Negroes. Escaping slaves, picking their way along darkened trails toward the North Star, felt they were sure to make it to freedom when they reached the wide Ohio River. Now, more than a hundred years later, crossing the Ohio meant for a young black boy that soon he would reach a playground where he could climb and slide, where he could swing so high that it felt like he could almost stretch out his toes and reach the sky.

Sometimes there were political discussions in my house that centered on race, I recall, discussions among my parents and their friends, generally people who had something to do with one or another of the colleges. Civil rights was very much a shared enterprise, and it seemed that everyone felt a part of the struggle—and that everyone had an opinion about how it should proceed. The adults would talk about Roy Wilkins of the NAACP, whom they all liked, and about Martin Luther King, the firebreathing Baptist preacher about whom not everybody agreed; for some, he was too rough, too insistent, and brashly had had the temerity to usurp leadership from Wilkins and Whitney Young and the others who'd spent longer, harder years toiling in the vineyard. I remember talk about the March on Washington, about John Kennedy and Thurgood Marshall and somebody we didn't like at all named That Old Segregationist Strom Thurmond, or sometimes, if he had done something especially outrageous and obnoxious, That Damn Old Segregationist Cracker Strom Thurmond. Politics and the promise of change were in the air. Even as a child I had a sense of where we stood in American society, or where people had decided we were supposed to stand, and how desperately that standing had to be made to change.

But what I don't remember feeling is any constant, day-to-day sense of our family's being personally oppressed. The resentment and the sense of injustice were always present, but the actual rage, the kind that debilitates and corrodes, appeared only in flashes. But those flashes could light up the night sky. Once, we were out for a drive and my grandmother needed to use the rest room. When she was shown to a gas station's dank "colored" restroom around back, dirty and smell and humiliating, my father came back to the car with an anger in his eyes that frightened me. I'm sure my parents must have sheltered me from many other such humiliations, but the truth is that I remember relatively few. If rage eats away at the soul, then we were remarkably uncorroded.

The reason, I see looking back, is that when everybody's black, nobody's black. To be black in America, when I was growing up, was to be treated as second-class compared to whites. But most of the time I didn't compare myself to whites at all. There was no reason to. All the relatives I knew, all the family friends, all the teachers and the preachers, the artists, the scholars, the traveling salesmen and the Methodist deacons and the street-corner bums, all the people in my world considered themselves Negro or colored. Most of the outside world doubtless looked at me in racial terms, but most of the time that wasn't the way I looked back. It sounds like I'm saying my world was colorless, but that's not the case at all. Rather, my world was in its entirety a world of color. It was all around me, and trying to see it was like trying to see air.

I DIDN'T SEE color very clearly in Orangeburg, but I did see class.

We lived at the corner of Boulevard and Oak, in an ample two-story house. Across Oak lived Mrs. Daisy Taylor, a friend of my grandmother's, and later Arthur Rose, a noted artist who taught at Claflin, and his family. Next door on Oak lived the Greens. I don't recall what George Green did for a living, but his wife, Ida Mae, worked in the student center at State College. Next to them were the Baileys; he was a cobbler and she a seamstress. Next door on Boulevard, in a little house our family owned, lived a succession of tenants, and next door to them lived Alec Lewis, who did something at State, his wife, Alba, the seventh- and eighth-grade teacher at Felton, and their son, Mickey, with whom I had to play very carefully—no hitting or wrestling—because he was a hemophiliac. Next to the Lewises was Mr. Thomas, a confirmed bachelor who lived alone and played the organ at Trinity Methodist Church—our church, down the street. Farther past Mr. Thomas lived Mrs. Harrington, another friend of my grandmother's.

This was our set of people in the neighborhood, and they were apart from the families who lived farther down Oak Street, poor families who lived in tumbledown little houses with mangy dogs in the yard, families with absent fathers and no visible means of support. These people lived just a few hundred yards away, and I didn't know them. I knew *of* them, vaguely. I knew to avoid their dogs when I walked down the street to the playground, and I knew them enough to wave at a familiar face as I passed, but I didn't know them as people.

In my backyard stood a huge old oak tree, garlanded with thick wisteria vines. I was a big fan of the Tarzan movies that played on television on Saturdays, and so every day I'd go out back and swing on the vines and give the Tarzan yell at the top of my lungs, loud enough and long enough to call an elephant. One day, a kid down at the end of the street yelled back in response. From then on, every once in a while when I yelled, the kid would yell back. But I never met him. I wasn't a particularly shy child, but it didn't occur to me that I would somehow become friends with a boy who lived down at the end of Oak Street. It wasn't forbidden or anything, it just didn't seem likely. It didn't fit into my view of the world.

Perhaps this sounds as if I grew up in some sort of bubble of wealth, and that's not really true. None of us in my family's circle of friends had any real money. But we did have education and we did have ambition, and in these things we were different from many other black people in the South. We were different from Miss Birdie and Mr. Major, for example, a middle-aged couple who we'd occasionally visit. They lived in the country, on a little farm; that was where I first saw pigs, first tried to pet a mule, first used an outhouse. They were poor and unlearned, they had fewer teeth than they should have had, and their hands were gnarled and calloused from their lifetimes of hard labor. They lived among earthy smells, among big wallowing hogs and preening roosters, among mud and muck and mire. For a skinny kid with soft hands and buckteeth and glasses, going out to their farm was like going to another world.

It's not as if I didn't have regular contact with poor people; the various economic strata of our black community, like those of any black community in those days, were held together by the external pressure of segregation. At the barbershop, in the chair to your right might be the president of State College, who lived in a fine new house with more rooms than any family could ever use, and in the chair to your left might be a gardener or a gas jockey or one of Orangeburg's few genuine bums. I knew the difference, knew that there was something that distinguished us from one another. At church each Sunday I'd politely say hello to old men who'd been wearing the same shiny black suit for more years than I could count.

Religion itself had its own connotations of class, especially for people of a certain age. The pecking order in the black church was remarkably like that of the white church, with a few variations. My grandmother—everybody called her "Miss Sadie"—and the ladies of her generation at our church felt that Episcopalians were stiff and snooty, with their dry homilies and rhythmless hymns. They were seen as, or thought to see themselves as, some sort of upper crust. Baptists, on the other hand, were seen to be poorer, less educated, perhaps a little coarser. There was something overly common about the way they went about the business of worship. Sadie and her friends thought that Baptists were way over the top, with their loud gospel shouting and their fainting in the aisles and their singsong, call-and-response sermons that could last the whole morning. Pentecostals, who spoke in tongues and were reliably reported to roll around on the floor, were considered simply beyond the pale. Roman Catholics were ritualistic and bizarre, mumbling in Latin, crossing themselves constantly, taking communion every day instead of just on the first Sunday of the month; old Mrs. Bailey from down the street was a Catholic, and I remember seeing her every morning as she trudged slowly past the house, rain or shine, on her way to Mass.

We Methodists were right in the middle, as far as my grandmother's generation was concerned. Trinity Methodist Church was a middle-class institution, a solid brick edifice with well-kept grounds and a huge stained-glass window behind the altar and a full basement for suppers to mark weddings and funerals. We went every Sunday, sitting in the same pews but not together: my grandmother with her friends, my great-aunt Florella with hers, my mother and father in the right transept, my sister and I in other parts of the church with kids in our age groups. For many years Miss Sadie had played piano at Sunday services. At various times, we all sang in various choirs. We had our tried and true spirituals (Negro spirituals, not gospel; there's a big difference, as anyone who's ever sung in a black church choir can tell you) and we had our heartfelt sermons that made you feel the spirit. But unlike in a Baptist church, the preacher still got you home at a reasonable hour for Sunday dinner.

In black Orangeburg we separated ourselves according to income and religion. Looking back, I can see now that at least to some extent we also sorted ourselves according to color.

This was particularly difficult for me to see at the time because of my own family's makeup, descended as we were from coal and cream. My immediate family consists of four distinctly different colors: Ellen is darkest, a rich cocoa brown; then my mother, a kind of milk chocolate; then my father, maple-toned; and then me. My grandmother, Sadie Smith, who lived with us in the house her father built, was darker than Ellen. My great-aunt, Florella Fordham, who also lived with us in her childhood home, was about the same shade as me, perhaps a bit lighter. There was no reason for me to think of this variety as other than the natural order of things, so that within the context of "colored" I never gave color a serious thought.

But now, if I do think about color in those days, I can see a clear pattern. My friends and their families generally ranged from milk chocolate to café au lait in complexion, a wide range, but generally on one side of some dividing line. The poor people who lived in Sunnyside and out in the country and at the end of Oak Street tended to be darker. In Brazil, they would have been the almost midnights and the after midnights and the navy blues. This was far from an absolute rule, but when I think of the girls at Felton who were thought to be beautiful — Maria Dawson and Penny Dawkins, with their long wavy hair, Toni Whaley, with her hazel eyes, Melissa Evans, with her pretty smile — I realize that they were all light-skinned. Black hadn't become beautiful just yet.

This is embarrassing to recall, because it wasn't supposed to be that way. Orangeburg was basically a community of old-school intellectuals; I hardly recall visiting a house during my childhood that didn't have shelves groaning with encyclopedias and atlases and Great Books. We were smart enough and politically conscious enough to realize that the black-white divide was the only one that mattered, that racial identity had to be accompanied by solidarity if we were ever to fight our way out from under Jim Crow and Johnny Reb. And we did have solidarity, tons of it.

The Bythewood family, for example, that lived across the railroad tracks on Goff Avenue—T. K. the undertaker, Emmie his wife, daughter Alvin, and son T. K. Junior—looked white. Granted, they looked white with an asterisk: A careful ethnologist equipped with a color-measuring densitometer could have spotted the telltale brownish undertones in their skin instead of pinkish. But a man from Mars, and certainly a man from Brazil, would have called them white. Yet they were Negroes—and proudly so—with no pretense or aspiration of being anything else. Undertakers tend to be both prominent and affluent in black communities, and so the Bythewoods did pretend to a certain status, but always within the context of black Orangeburg, Negro Orangeburg. Likewise the Washingtons and the Sultons, various of whom could have "passed" with little trouble if they'd been so inclined. But we stuck together, ignoring the evidence of the color wheel as both irrelevant and distracting.

Yet at the end of the day there was a correlation that any statistician would probably have found significant. Our socioeconomic ladder was a stubby one, with few rungs. But clustered near the top were a mixed bag of generally lighter tones, and clustered near the bottom were the darkest tones of all. Looking back over the decades I have to conclude there was some dynamic at work there, some dynamic that I didn't recognize at all at the time, that I only began to see after I'd spent time in Brazil, and that I'm still not sure I completely understand.

THERE WERE TWO high schools in Orangeburg when I was growing up, as in most southern towns, the white high school and the black high school. More than a decade after the *Brown* v. *Board of Education* decision had theoretically ended the fiction of separate-but-equal schooling and opened up all the schools in the nation, all-white Orangeburg High began admitting its first black students. I entered the tenth grade in 1967 as part of the second or third wave of blacks — or rather the second or third wavelet, since we were just a handful.

I came in with an attitude and with something to prove, an attitude provoked by not being wanted. But this was also the autumn after the Summer of Love. Compared to San Francisco, the city I kept reading about and dreaming about, Orangeburg seemed on a different planet, a planet where nobody wore flowers in their hair and nothing was even remotely groovy. But I was aware of what was going on out there in the world, and like most young people across the country I wanted to feel a part of it.

One characteristic of the Movement was a blurring of racial lines. Jimi Hendrix was black but he was playing rock and roll; Janis Joplin was white but she was singing the blues. *Everybody get together, come and love one another right now.* So I let my own racial identity blur — or, at least I felt, inside, as if I were letting it blur. I listened to hippie music and read *The Strawberry Statement* and tried to strike the correct hip poses. But I didn't know if I was doing it right. I didn't know exactly how to wear my faded blue jeans or which peace medallion was the coolest. There wasn't anybody around to talk about any of this stuff with. I felt like I was the only person in Orangeburg with a clue, and it wasn't much of a clue at that.

But then I found out that I wasn't alone. In my civics and history classes, where we often discussed politics, many of the white students faithfully parroted the John Birch–inspired ravings of their parents, while others espoused a kind of mainline conservatism, generally of the Dixiecrat persuasion. I was a lonely voice for what they called the "lub'rul" point of view, using the word like an epithet. But in our frequent arguments I noticed that another voice was reliably joining in on my side— Mike O'Cain's voice.

Mike was a doctor's son who'd grown up in a big white house, one of the stateliest old mansions in town, with big ante-bellum-style columns that made it look like a Hollywood set for a movie about the Old South. Despite the setting, though, Mike was not from central casting. His legs were weakened and slightly atrophied from a congenital nervous condition, so he walked jerkily and with difficulty. He was never going to be any good at football or baseball, the twin religions of the high school. Perhaps as a result of being shut out of the locker-room bonding rituals that were so big in the South, he seemed to like to think of himself as a proud outsider.

One day, while I was trying to hold my own in some argument about politics, Mike jumped in on my side. The next day, as he was being harangued, I jumped in on his. We developed the habit of helping each other, and gradually that led to the habit of friendship. For the first time in my life, I had a white friend.

We'd talk at school, hang out together, plot to leave our mark on some school institution or another that we found hidebound and ridiculous, help each other study for exams, scheme to foment our own little revolution, talk on the phone. Then one day came the unexpected, almost the unimaginable: Mike invited me to his house.

Mike wanted me to come over to listen to his Bob Dylan records. To this day I'm convinced that we were the only two people within a good forty miles who knew who Bob Dylan was.

I had never been to a white classmate's house before, but I couldn't see any reasons not to go, so I found myself one evening heading for the O'Cain mansion with a mixture of pride, militance, trepidation, and awe. I remember walking into that amazing house, its every column and staircase and chandelier a symbol of a time when white meant master and black meant slave, and thinking that perhaps our society had come further than I'd realized, if someone like me could walk through the front door of a place like that. We went up to his room and sat there listening to "Subterranean Homesick Blues" and talking about what fools and dolts and idiots many of our classmates were, and for that evening we created a society of two in which blackness or whiteness just didn't seem to matter at all. We allowed ourselves to believe there were many, many more important things in this kaleidoscopic world than our ancient and foolish quarrels over a discredited anthropological concept called race.

I was soon disabused of this dangerous idea.

In February 1968—February of the year when so many things happened in America, so many assassinations and riots and upheavals that we forget half of them—students at South Carolina State and Claflin tried to integrate a pitiful, scummy little whites-only bowling alley called the All-Star Lanes in downtown Orangeburg, not far from the Winn-Dixie grocery store, just down the street from the Piggly Wiggly with its logo of a smiling porker.

The owner resisted, and what had begun as a protest over the right to enter one insignificant little segregated business turned into a more general airing of pent-up grievances. The protests grew angrier and angrier over several nights, and the city's white authorities grew increasingly nervous. The whole town was tense, and I remember having the feeling, for the first time in my life, but not the last, that something really bad was about to happen.

The authorities decided that since there had "never been no trouble" in Orangeburg before, the protests must be the work of those shadowy, probably communist, definitely Yankee-inspired operatives that white folks throughout the Civil Rights–era South had come to call "outside agitators."

And they believed they'd found one, an actual outside agitator, in the person of Cleveland Sellers, a young organizer for the "militant" Student Non-Violent Coordinating Committee. He was far from being the Lenin that the Orangeburg police thought he was, but there was no denying that he'd been agitating for SNCC on the South Carolina State and Claflin campuses. Clevie Sellers had been living in a house across the railroad tracks from Claflin—three doors down from my house.

That was why I awoke one morning, two or three days into the protests, to find a row of a dozen Highway Patrol cars parked across from my house, doors open, officers crouched behind the doors, rifles trained on the house where Clevie Sellers lived—or had lived. He had long since left town, but the image of those troopers, crouched and ready to fire, remains.

That was the morning when, for the first time, I felt vulnerable. That was when I first felt the need for race to be a more aggressive defense against the white world. It was an awakening, my first glimpse of the lengths to which some elements in the South were willing to go to resist change.

The protests reached their climax with a nighttime standoff, two days later, on the wide strip of railroad tracks and sidings that ran between the two side-by-side campuses and the street where I lived. The police would later claim that someone in the crowd had fired first, but this was never proved. Whatever the spark, the police and patrolmen began firing, and within minutes three students lay dying—their names were Smith, Hammond, and Middleton—wounded, among other places, in their backs and in the soles of their feet.

The students were black, the men who shot them white. This took place within a hundred yards of my house, with a clear line of sight.

Suddenly race once again mattered to me, and mattered a great deal. There was no outward change—I doubt that any of my friends or even my family noticed the change that I so clearly felt. But I felt it nonetheless. The only concrete manifestation was that for a while, at least, I spent less time trying to learn about the Summer of Love and more reading about the Black Panthers and considering the ramifications of Black Power. I had learned a lesson: that when tempers rise and bullets fly, black men's bodies somehow always seem to get in the way. For all the emphasis that society claimed to place on attitude or education or affluence, it was still, in the end, a matter of biology. I learned that since I was black, I could never, ever be white.

I could hang out with Mike O'Cain, I could be friends with Mike O'Cain, I could have the same opinions and the same interests as Mike O'Cain, but I would never, ever be *the same as Mike O'Cain.*

A COUPLE OF years later I left to go off to school in Ann Arbor, Michigan. I left my snug black cocoon for the wider world, meaning the white world.

Except for visits, I've never really gone back. My studies have been at white universities; my jobs have been with white institutions; I have close white friends. I know the white idiom as well as the black. I speak a neutral and unaccented anchorman's English; and I have as many brain cells uselessly dedicated to retaining Led Zeppelin guitar solos—hell, even Simon and Garfunkel lyrics—as I do to Smokey Robinson songs and George Clinton riffs. I move easily and un-self-consciously in white America.

Ellen would later make a different choice. She'd had the same upringing I had; she'd gone to the same school, suffered and excelled under the same teachers, listened to the same sermons every Sunday, but in the end decided to conduct her life in a "blacker" context. She went to Spelman College in Atlanta, one of the premier black schools. She joined Delta Sigma Theta, one of the leading black sororities. She emerged with a passionate commitment to the survival of historically black colleges and universities nationwide and to the idea that a setting in which African Americans learn with other African Americans, from other African Americans, has immense, enduring value. It was the subject of her Ph.D. thesis, and it's a passion that she puts into practice every day now with her students in the business school at South Carolina State. For a long time I didn't really understand. For a long time I thought she was putting artificial restraints on her life—blinders, governors, hobbles—that would have been easy to leave aside.

And yet never again, after that February day in Orangeburg, did I entertain the notion that race was something I could just ignore. It might be closer to the surface of my life during some periods, and tamped further down at others, but it's always there, every step of the way. The question is how to deal with it: how to cut it down to size, how to keep it in perspective, how to keep from being crushed by it. How to live with it.

Now I'd come to South America. Thousands of miles from home, on the wrong side of the equator, I was looking for a new way—even a host of new ways—to coexist with this overbearing presence. Brazil, for the first time, offered me hope.

Even a middle-of-the-road, lapsed Methodist like me wanted to shout Hallelujah!

Chapter 4

Invisibility

BRAZIL WAS MY LOVE, MY INSPIRATION, MY REVELATION. BUT I traveled around the rest of the South American continent as well, and saw other variations on the theme of race that would never have occurred to me back home. My job, after all, boiled down to three imperatives: travel, observe, and write. Flitting in and out of these societies, I truly felt like a fly on the wall, an irrelevance, a nonparticipant, an onlooker who saw but was not seen. I thought of Ralph Ellison: I felt truly invisible.

Peru was one example, a complex and fascinating society, a civilization of almost Egyptian antiquity now reduced to grinding but proud poverty. Peru was a racial stew, but one with its own unique proportions and spices, and its own challenges to my way of seeing the world.

Lima is smelly and scummy and overcrowded, always overcast and gloomy, numbingly poor, a hard city to love. But I fell in love with the place one day when I was walking to visit some friends in a fairly upscale residential district, rounded a corner without paying much attention to where I was going, and literally stumbled into a pyramid. It was a couple of thousand years old, eroded into a mound that only suggested its former shape, but did so unmistakably. The site had been the source of many artifacts, and there were probably more to find, but the government had no money for continued excavation and so there it stood, in the middle of an ordinary neighborhood, without even so much as a sign explaining what it was. You could walk over and scoop up a handful of history and let it run through your fingers.

In another part of town there was a grove of ancient olive trees. They were not like any olive trees I'd ever seen, but rather big, thick, gnarly things, with huge twisted trunks and thick spiky branches that seemed full of menace. Legend had it that they had been planted by one of Pizarro's men right after the conquest. The legend might have been apocryphal, but you could walk among those trees and imagine some sixteenth-century Spaniard, doubtless a brawling hell-raiser from Extremadura who'd fought for and won a new life as a colonial gentleman, laying out his orchard and calculating the years until his first harvest.

It was on my third or fourth trip to Lima that it dawned on me that the staff at my regular hotel had a distinct pecking order, based on color.

The men and women who worked behind the reception desk and in the administrative offices were all white, with European features and extremely fair skin, descendants of that Spaniard who planted the olive trees. The men who did the menial work, who made up all the beds and changed the towels and vacuumed the hallways, were all Indian, every single one of them, descendants of the people who built that pyramid around the corner. And the doormen were all extremely tall and slim—and extremely black, of African descent.

In time I had occasion to stay at other hotels, and I was struck at how the pattern never varied. Whites were in the high-value-added jobs, the white-collar positions that were routinely advertised in the classified as being open only to those with *"buena presencia"*—"good presence," a euphemism for white skin. Black-haired, red-brown-skinned Indians occupied the menial jobs and did the dirty work. And Afro-Peruvians occupied a bizarre niche that's hard to describe, a kind of intermediate role that was something like window dressing. In a mixed and mangled racial metaphor, I came to think of Afro-Peruvians as living, breathing, cigar-store Indians—or maybe, more to the point, as living, breathing lawn jockeys.

Black men stood at attention in front of the luxury hotels, resplendent as peacocks and only slightly ridiculous in their bright-red uniforms studded with dazzling brass buttons. Black security guards stood menacingly in front of banks and other businesses, protection against the guerrillas and the bandits and the utter chaos of Lima, their Uzis well-oiled and their military-style berets cocked at a jaunty angle. Standing outside with an authoritative air was something that black people, for some reason, were seen as being very good at.

Blacks also performed another, more lugubrious, public role: Whenever a prominent Peruvian died, a titan of industry or a sage of the law or whatever, the first thing his family did in planning the funeral was to hire a corps of black pallbearers to carry the casket in the procession. Peru is in many ways an exotic place with many unusual customs, but this was truly one of the weirdest rituals I've ever encountered anywhere in the world. The whole point, the only point, was to have black men — African-featured, kinky-haired men — bearing the deceased on their broad shoulders. It didn't matter that the deceased wouldn't have known those men in life, or, for that matter, that the deceased and his family and everyone else attending the funeral were white or mestizo. You couldn't plant a leading light, or someone who had pretensions as a leading light, without a bunch of black guys to send him off.

I spent a lot of time in Peru over the years, and this odd status held by black folks — specifically, black men — was puzzling to me. Afro-Peruvians clearly did not have anything near the economic or social status of whites, and yet in some contexts they seemed to be accorded a bit more respect than the dark-skinned Indian majority.

I was especially confused by the reaction I sometimes got when I went places where the demographic was purely Indian.

I recall my first trip to the shantytown called Huaycan. Clinging to a completely barren hillside just outside the city, Huaycan was one of literally hundreds of squatter settlements that ringed Lima, filled mostly with Indians from the highlands driven to the capital by poverty and political violence. Huaycan was interesting because it was being infiltrated by the Shining Path guerrillas, a band of bloodthirsty pseudo-Maoists who at that time were perilously close to taking over the whole country. My reason for going to the shantytown was to try to talk to a brave community leader who was standing up to the rebels — and who, for her courage, was almost certain to be killed.

I didn't have any contacts in Huaycan, so I went in cold, driving my rented car past row after row of improvised dwellings, the most recent arrivals living in lean-tos made of straw mats, the more established residents in houses of cinderblock or brick. Not a single building was complete, because nobody could afford to buy more than a few blocks or bricks at a time, bringing them home on foot or by bus if necessary.

I stopped at the first house where I saw activity, and the reaction of the woman inside, predictably, was wariness—she didn't want to talk to any stranger with a funny accent. I recall what she was doing, though: folding a daughter's perfectly laundered and pressed school uniform. The nearest source of water was the Rimac River, a good kilometer away, and the Rimac's water was putrid; I've always wondered how she got that uniform blouse so white, and how she ironed the skirt's pleats so perfectly, in a one-room shack with a dirt floor and no water or power.

I walked up the main drag, past improvised bars and bodegas and a little cinderblock church and, as I might have predicted, nobody was anxious to talk to me. But there was something else in the air that I hadn't predicted. I sensed an edge of hostility that I didn't understand, that seemed to go well beyond the caution of an embattled community toward an uninvited stranger. Some of the men I passed gave me aggressive, stare-down looks. A couple of them bumped me deliberately. I never did find the community leader I was looking for, and eventually I gave up and left, deciding this just wasn't the kind of place I was going to weasel into without knowing somebody. Unlike much of Lima, this place wasn't the least bit cosmopolitan; these were recent arrivals to the big city, men and women pretty much straight from the highlands, and for some reason they didn't seem to like me.

I got a similar reaction once when I was strolling through a rural handicrafts market high in the Andes, a surprising hint of aggression that seemed to be fueled by resentment—a half-sneer, a stare whose duration offered a challenge, a shoulder turned coldly. What, I asked myself, did I ever do to these people to deserve being treated like this?

Plenty, it turned out. A historian I met in Lima filled me in on the background: Many blacks were brought to Peru as slaves and some others arrived as free men, but all were considered by the Spanish colonial overlords to be much more acculturated—and thus much more civilized, or at least civilizable—than the Indian natives. Because of this, blacks were often employed as plantation overseers whose task was to keep the Indian laborers in line, to literally crack the whip while the Indians picked the cotton. Down through the decades and centuries that relationship seemed to have left its attenuated trace.

Knowing that history meant that Peru suddenly had a new way of holding my interest. It was a multiracial society where history saved its worst disadvantages for a group other than mine—and perhaps even gave the slightest little relative boost to people who looked like me. This was something I'd never experienced before.

At first it was a sinful pleasure, one that in retrospect I'm a bit ashamed of. I came closer than I like to admit to actually enjoying that look of apprehension and resentment that I sometimes provoked in people, and I definitely enjoyed the feeling of entitlement, however small and fleeting, that I sometimes let myself experience. When society mandates that you belong on the bottom layer, you feel like you've got to have solidarity with anybody and everybody. When you're not, you can afford to be more selective about the people you include in the pronoun "we"—in fact, you're obliged to *want* to be selective. The whole point of not being on the bottom is to be able to be selective. Layered on top of this was the fact that I was an American and the fact that an aura of power and wealth inevitably surrounded any American in these parts. At times it was heady: swagger through town, stare at anybody you want to stare at, stare them down, and to hell with what the Indians think.

It was a fleeting and empty triumph, though, because ultimately I couldn't escape the obvious parallel. In Peru and the rest of the Andean countries it was impossible for me to see how dark-skinned Indians were treated and not empathize. I learned that, in the final analysis, I make a lousy overlord.

WHAT WAS INTERESTING about South America was the opportunity it gave me to observe discrimination from the outside, with some measure of objectivity. It was like keeping a log of a scientific experiment, another version of the white-black relationship I'd grown up with in the United States—lighter-skinned people, in control of political and economic resources, looking down on darker-skinned people. But there was one big difference: In South America I was a kind of neutral observer, able to eavesdrop on both white people and "colored folks," positioned to see and hear things I'd never be allowed to witness at home.

In a wealthy suburb of Lima, a few days before an election in which the Indian majority was clearly about to take the white elite down a few pegs, I sat in the living room of a society matron and listened politely as she explained that the Indians in the villages and the shantytowns simply weren't qualified to vote. They just didn't have the knowledge or the intelligence. She used a word, *cholo*, that means "dark-skinned" but has an insulting, pejorative sense, like the word "darkie" must have sounded in its heyday. She told me she immensely resented the prospect of being forced to respect and obey a president chosen by *them*.

I listened politely, and nodded, and wondered: Is this, for example, the way white Chicagoans would have talked the week before Harold Washington was elected mayor?

In Chile, another country where the basic racial issue was white versus Indian, I once attended a wildly enthusiastic—almost sexually frenzied—women's political rally for a man not ordinarily known for driving the ladies wild: General Augusto Pinochet. The old buzzard was more popular among Chile's upper classes than most people realize, and certain wealthy women responded to his silver hair and his gold-braid-festooned white uniform the way others responded to the aging Sinatra in his tux. By the time he took the stage, I thought they were ready to start throwing their panties.

On closer inspection, it turned out that the crowd was made up of two distinct kinds of women: affluent white matrons, who favored the order and prosperity Pinochet had brought to the country, and their darker-skinned Indian maids, who'd been given the afternoon off and ordered to accompany their *señoras* to the rally so as to pad the numbers and make more of an impression for the eleven o'clock news. The scene, at least for me, had the feel of the segregated American South, a kind of Miss Daisy feel. Mistress and servant.

I talked to a few of the ladies, bedecked in their tailored outfits and their fiery diamonds and their neck-straining ropes of gold, and they went on at length about Pinochet and what a great man he was and how the things we foreigners had heard and written about Chile were all wrong and how all the people really loved him. Then they tugged forth the dark-skinned maids at their sides, Carmen and Maria and Luisa, so that I could hear that message straight from the little people themselves. The maids reminded me of those poor souls brought forth during the civil rights movement days to tell the so-called Yankee interlopers that poll taxes and the like were just fine with them: "No, Massa, Ol' Joe don' care nuthin' 'bout no votin'."

The maids told me, dutifully and with apparent sincerity, that they loved the ground that the old butcher Pinochet walked on. As soon as the *señora* looked away, though, they gave me a thumbs-down or held their noses or made some other signal to let me know what they really thought.

"The old son of a bitch," one of them told me. "We're all voting to throw him out. We're voting against *them.*"

She had used the feminine form of the pronoun "them." She meant the mistresses, all the Miss Daisies of Chile. A few weeks later, these dark maids thronged the polling places and finally booted the old general out of the presidential palace.

That rally was held in Viña del Mar, a fabled old resort town on the Chilean coast. Later that night I found myself walking the darkened streets of the town, essentially killing time until the hour when I was supposed to meet my ride back to Santiago, the capital.

My senses were all heightened, as was always the case when I had to navigate unfamiliar terrain at night; every creak of a doorway, every clack of a pedestrian's step, every shadowy motion at the periphery of my vision was sharp and immediate. I never had any trouble, walking these dicey cities after dark. Then again, I never was less than alert. I always watched for little anomalies, which could be dangerous—and suddenly, one such anomaly caught my eye. Up ahead, well in the distance but coming my way, a looming figure approached, a dim silhouette completely out of scale with my expectations.

This silhouetted man was absurdly taller than most Chileans. His walk, too, had an anomalous gait, one that struck my eye as inappropriate yet somehow familiar. It was very dark and I couldn't make out anything else about him, but our paths were about to cross. Involuntarily, I folded myself into the no-interaction, no-eye-contact, don't-mess-with-me posture of the urban survivor.

The man loped closer, until we passed on the narrow sidewalk. My peripheral vision caught an unexpected image, one it took me a while to process. He was quicker. We were already past each other, separating, when I heard a voice say, in English, "How you doin', man?"

That stopped me dead in my tracks. I looked back and saw a young black man, roughly six feet six inches tall, wearing a black leather jacket and toting a big gym bag.

"What's happening?" I said.

"How you doin' man?" he repeated.

Then I blurted out: "What the hell are *you* doing here?"

"Back at you," he said. "I live here, and I can tell you, you don't see many of *us* on the street, you know what I mean? Welcome to Chile."

There are essentially no black people in Chile—even fewer than in Argentina. In all my previous trips the only black faces I'd seen had been a couple of marines at the U.S. embassy and the man in the mirror. Full stop.

This black man's name was Terry Jones, and he was on his way to play a basketball game. He asked what I was doing in Chile, and I told him. We talked for a few minutes, both of us enjoying the novelty if nothing else, and then he said he was sorry but he really had to run or else he'd be late. Did I want to come along?

I had nothing more urgent to do, and so I walked with him until we reached a nondescript metal door that led down a dark hallway. At the end, we emerged into a tight little gymnasium, with high-school-style bleachers that held a modest smattering of basketball fans; we had come in via the players' entrance, and this was a scheduled contest in the Chilean professional basketball league.

There were only a handful of fans, which was just as well, since the gym was smaller than that of the average American high school, its bleachers about as commodious. There was so little room behind the baskets that anyone who dared a fast break would be in serious danger of slamming into the end wall. There didn't seem to be any dressing rooms; Terry went right to his team's bench, sat down, and took off his sweats, revealing that he was already wearing his uniform. I took a seat near mid-court.

The arena had all the electricity and excitement of, well, maybe an off-season practice. Terry's coach lectured the team nonstop until tip-off time. The ref blew the whistle, the teams took the court, and the game began.

Basketball is enough of a universal language that I was able to suss out what was going on fairly easily. Terry's was the home team, substantially more talented and better coached than the competition. Terry was the star of his squad, as was his black American counterpart on the other team; the most exciting action consisted of these two Americans going after each other, with drives and dunks and steals and all, while their teammates stood around and watched. The Chilean players who rounded out the teams were enthusiastic, and perfectly capable of making an un-molested set shot, but not nearly as gifted or skilled as Terry and the other American guy.

Because of their obvious superiority, each of the Americans was the focus of the other team's defensive strategy, which was, essentially, foul hard and foul often. The Americans were scoring the lion's share of the points, but they were also getting banged around mercilessly, with elbows and forearms and knees. The officials did nothing to help them, keeping their silence even at the most egregious fouls. In part, this doubtless was due to sheer incompetence and gross unfamiliarity with the game. But there also seemed to be a nationalistic agenda at work here, a desire to give the plucky little Chileans some chance of competing against the big, bad, black Yankees.

The two hundred or so spectators who had come to see the game obviously were enjoying it—they yelled and screamed like basketball fans anywhere in the world—but in truth it was a boring game, and I needed to get back to my hotel room in Santiago. So at halftime I went over to say good-bye to Terry. He said he was sorry we hadn't had more time to talk, and he gave me his phone number.

"Please call, okay?" he said.

A few days later, after it had become clear that news would keep me in Chile at least another week, I called Terry and arranged to visit him and his family. I was curious: Here in a place where, as I knew from personal experience, a black man was treated like a Martian, what kind of life could he possibly have?

It turned out that he lived in one of the pricey high-rises near the beach. When I rang the buzzer, a male voice answered in Spanish. I was caught short, until I recognized the voice as Terry's. "Hey!" he said. "Come on up."

It wasn't Terry who came to the door, but his wife, Yvonne, a pretty woman of slender build and average Chilean height, about five-two, with tawny skin, curly brown hair, and laughing eyes. She welcomed me in Spanish, and then Terry came around the corner, all six-six of him. He shook my hand warmly, introduced

Yvonne, and then had a brief exchange with her in Spanish; I didn't catch much of it, but it seemed to be about the meal they were planning to serve. Terry showed me into the living room and, waiting there for us, looking up with a smile from Terry's favorite chair, was a curly-haired toddler with light-brown skin — their son, Thomas.

I asked Terry about his life in Chile, and he needed no further prompting. For the next few hours, including over a lunch of Yvonne's entirely respectable southern fried chicken, I heard Terry's story.

He was twenty-six, and he was originally from Compton, having grown up there in the days before the name of the city came to connote death-wishing L.A. gangs and drive-by shootings. Back then it was just a striving black community still in the early stages of decline, a place were Bloods and Crips were just becoming commonplace in their all-red and all-blue ensembles, a place that a bright young man would size up as a place to leave far, far behind.

Terry had been a high-school basketball star, but not enough of a star to draw much interest from the big universities. He ended up going to a junior college and then transferring to Pan American University, a small school in Tulsa where they were delighted to have him play ball. His college playing career was a minor one and, not surprisingly, no one picked Terry in the National Basketball Association draft. He did get a few calls, however, from agents who wanted him to consider playing abroad. He attended a tryout camp for prospects who wanted to play in Europe, but wasn't chosen.

One persistent agent did call, however, with an offer to play in Chile. Terry barely knew where Chile was, but the offer to play there was the only one on the table. So he went.

The team wasn't in Santiago, the reasonably cosmopolitan capital, or even in Valparaíso, the second city, whose status as a bustling port gave it at least a whiff of other lands and other peoples. In fact, it wasn't even anywhere near Santiago, or Valparaíso, or any city anyone had ever heard of. Terry ended up in Curicó, a provincial town far to the south, playing basketball for a thousand dollars a month.

Few places are measurably closer to the end of the earth than Curicó, both physically and psychologically, and Terry Jones, with his size and his blackness, felt like the brother from another planet. He couldn't take it. After just four months, he fled back to Compton.

Whereupon he ran smack into the realities of life in urban America. Terry hadn't graduated from Pan American, and he wasn't basketball star anymore. He was just another tall black man without any money and without a college degree. He could get work loading trucks, but he hated it. He found a job with the recreation department supervising a playground, which he loved, since it gave him a chance to coach basketball, to be around the game that had meant so much to his life. But the gang situation was worsening, and the playgrounds were becoming battlegrounds for angry children who settled their disputes over thrown elbows and flagrant fouls with automatic weapons. Running a playground had become a dangerous job.

So Terry went back to Curicó, this time not an extraterrestrial dropping in for a quick visit but an extraterrestrial marooned, by choice, in a place that was many light-years from home.

He decided to make himself a life. Every night he took his dictionary to bed, teaching himself Spanish word by painstaking word, at a rate of precisely seven new words a night. Being able to communicate with the locals, even just a little, was good.

Even better: His eye was caught by a local girl named Yvonne who played with a volleyball team that practiced in the same Curicó gym that his basketball team used. They started dating, and as he came to know her family he grew more comfortable in his adopted country.

Marginally more comfortable, that is. He had to deal constantly with the fact that he was different, and the main difference was that his skin was a deep cocoa brown.

"Some of these towns where we went, they had never seen a black person before," Terry told me. "People would call, 'Hey, Blackie!' It took me a while to realize they didn't mean anything by it. One time, I heard a child ask his mother, 'Why is he so black? Doesn't he wash his face?'"

I kept asking how he managed to be so at ease, or at least to appear so at ease, in a place where he stood out so dramatically. I loved a lot of things about Chile, but I always felt so conspicuous there that it was difficult to really relax. The idea of living in Chile just seemed inconceivable to me.

Terry explained it in terms of options. In Compton, his color made him a candidate to become another grim statistic. In Chile, that same color made him conspicuous, yes, but also an instant celebrity. Within weeks of his arrival there wasn't a soul in Curicó who didn't know him by sight. He'd seen that not as a problem, but as a start.

By the time I'd met him he'd secured a better contract with the Valparaíso team—fifteen hundred a month, plus the apartment in Viña del Mar—and was full of plans. In the off-season he and Yvonne went back to Curicó, where he had a show on the local radio station, spinning rhythm and blues and sometimes rap. People loved it, even if they didn't understand a word of what the singers and rappers were saying. Terry wasn't making much money on the radio, but he saw possibilities. He wanted to get more into the media thing, maybe have a sports show on television.

Another possibility was to open a sporting-goods store, or preferably a string of sporting-goods stores; he'd observed that in Chile, at least, it was the capitalists rather than the wage earners who prospered. There was a slight problem, though: He didn't have any capital. He was trying to save, but it was hard with a family that simply needed certain things.

And he was beginning to miss Compton an awful lot. His budget didn't allow for frequent visits, so he missed his family. Maybe, someday, he would end up moving home.

When I left, I wasn't sure he'd follow through on any of his big dreams. But I was impressed at what he'd done with race, or rather what he'd done with his feelings about race. Talking to him I'd gotten the clear impression of a young man with a definite sense of race consciousness. Because of his situation, though, and because of his assessment of his present options, he'd put that consciousness on hold. He was keeping it in abeyance, because in his current circumstances it would have been a hindrance rather than a help. To feel injured by every slight, to feel oppressed or insulted by every stare, would have left him paralyzed.

He'd decided, simply, to deny race and color their destructive power. But at the same time, he'd decided to use them to his best advantage. Rather than hide from being the equivalent of a sideshow attraction, he'd exploited that status to achieve minor celebrity, a radio show, and business prospects that went well beyond those he might have expected to line up back home in Compton. He'd learned to make race sometimes work for him, not always against him.

I saw Terry's life almost as a kind of parable. He'd never even been to Brazil, but he'd learned to do what the Brazilians did: He took his race off and put it on as it suited him, depending on the circumstances. He ignored it, he willed it away, and then he summoned it back when he wanted or needed to. What was wrong with that? Why shouldn't we all live like that?

He did seem a little lonely, though, and an awfully long way from home.

Chapter 5

Absence of Malice

I WAS RUSHING THROUGH THE CROWDS OF OF SÃO PAULO'S MAIN financial district one day, late for an interview with a banker, when I reached a bottleneck. There was construction underway at the modern art museum, and the workmen had commandeered and blocked off about half the width of the sidewalk, which was already much too narrow to handle the flow of office workers, messengers, millionaires, tramps, pickpockets, and other enterprising souls drawn to the South American equivalent of Wall Street. For a stretch of about fifteen feet the sidewalk was so narrow that it was impossible for two people to pass. Like traffic on a country lane that crosses a one-lane bridge, eastbound and westbound pedestrians had to alternate if anyone was going to get anywhere.

The woman in front of me got her chance to dash through the narrow stretch, and then a young man came through from the other side, and then it was my turn. But as I started ahead, a businessman came charging through toward me.

He was middle-aged, silver-haired, well-dressed, white by any standards, and clearly in a big hurry. He was also extremely impolite. *"Com licença,"* he said—"With permission," a standard Brazilian excuse-me—but he growled the words in a way that changed their meaning to something like "Get the hell out of my way."

I took another step forward, my jaw suddenly clenching, my shoulders and gut tensing for the confrontation—and then I realized where I was. I stopped, took two steps back, and let the man pass. Despite his obnoxiousness, I might even have tipped my hat to him if I'd been wearing one. I was late for my appointment, which was both an embarrassment and an inconvenience, but nevertheless I was in a good mood for the rest of the day. Because I hadn't had to get mad.

In America I'd have been obliged to take offense. That businessman wouldn't have been just a boor who'd tried to bully his way through out of turn. He'd have been a *white* man who'd tried to take some discernible advantage, however slight, of me, a *black* man, and I'd have been forced to make an issue of that. Not to get physical or anything, of course, and probably not even to say anything about it. But I would have had to make it at least a private issue, one that I'd stew on for at least a few minutes, maybe even a few hours, and I'd have had to get angry. It's axiomatic for any black American, especially for any black American man, that if you're slighted by a white person, especially a white American man, you have to feel at least some measure of anger about it—racial anger.

And this was difficult for me. It was one of those areas of direct conflict between my private nature and my public—my public what? *Duty* sounds much too strong, but that's really what it was, my duty to feel the anger of the ages.

All my life I've hated anger and loathed confrontation. There was never very much of either in my house when I was growing up in Orangeburg; My parents are both even-tempered, my grandmother was always ready with some homespun saying to disarm any impending explosion, and aside from the usual sibling bouts between my sister and me, there was always a gentleness, and sometimes an indirectness, in the way we dealt with one another.

"Just as well laugh as to cry," my grandmother Sadie would say, and that pretty much summed up the family attitude. My mother, father, grandmother, and great-aunt all seemed utterly unflappable. Nobody screamed, nobody jumped up and down, nobody threw things. They seemed almost never to get mad, and when they did get mad they seemed never to stay mad for very long.

I realize now, of course, that they did get angry, like anyone else; the pressures of marriage, children, jobs, monthly bills, and the other elements of modern life always demand their tribute in frustration and rage. But if there was anger in Major Fordham's old house, and there must have been, then the adults took great pains to keep it out of sight and out of earshot of the children.

And so I drew lessons from all these adult examples of even-temperedness. I came to believe that anger was, somehow, a defeat. If you were provoked to the point of real anger, which involved a loss of control, then somehow you had been manipulated by circumstances. Things were running you instead of you running them. I learned to keep my anger inside so I could feel as if I were containing it, dominating it, conquering it—without realizing, of course, that it was still in there, accumulating and festering and building pressure. Inevitably, anger either corrodes or explodes.

I didn't even begin to learn how to get angry on a personal level until much later, after I had met Avis. She'd grown up in a household where people spoke their minds, to put it mildly, and didn't pull punches. Confronted with something that makes her mad, she blows up, and then the episode passes quickly, like a thunderstorm in July. I was shocked the first time she got mad at me over some trifle that I didn't even consider worth a raised eyebrow—I can't even remember anymore what it was—and then even more shocked when, just a few minutes later, the anger was completely gone. It was as if nothing had happened.

Avis was even more shocked, though, when she saw the results of my stick-it-in-the-closet approach. One evening, not that long after we'd met, we were sitting around her room in the Mission District of San Francisco and I was reading a book. I wasn't really paying much attention to her at that instant, and she felt like being paid attention to, and so she reached over and mischievously plucked off my glasses. Without my glasses I couldn't read. When I reached to take them back, she held them behind her back and darted away.

It was just a playful moment, totally innocent, nothing at all intended, lovers at play. But I went absolutely berserk. Within an instant I was almost blind with fury. I glowered and fumed and practically foamed at the mouth. Poor Avis was so stunned—I doubt she'd ever seen me even mildly cross before—that she walked out of her own house and went to a nearby park to wait until I'd left. It was many days and many plaintive phone calls before we made up.

And of course it hadn't been about the glasses. It had been the accumulation of things, all the little things that had made me mad for the past six months or two years or however long it had been since the previous explosion. I was yelling at Avis because a bus had splashed me with mud a few weeks earlier, and a copy editor had inserted a stupid mistake into one of my stories, and my boss had assigned me to another week of late shifts, and I'd ripped the pocket on my favorite pants, and the amount I thought I should have left in my checking account bore no relation to the amount the bank thought I should have. These things, and many more, had all piled up in a tremendous logjam—unremarked, unexamined—and then when Avis took off my glasses the jam broke loose and the flood ravaged all in its path. For me, anger equaled wanton destruction. I just didn't know how to get angry in a constructive way. It's taken me years to learn, and I'm still not that good at it.

At a fairly early age I did learn how to feel, and how to use, one specific kind of anger, though—racial anger. I knew our status in the South, and I was angry about it. I knew about the civil rights movement and the conditions that had made it necessary. I could recite all the relevant slogans. I knew about the Reverend Martin Luther King, Jr., and his gospel of nonviolence, but I was also aware of the existence of Malcolm X and his exhortation "by any means necessary." I knew about segregated bathrooms and reserved seats at the back of the bus. I knew about the nice playgrounds across town where I wasn't allowed to play, the new schools I wasn't allowed to attend. And I felt the roiling influence of history.

History imposes a heavy burden on the African-American man. Unfairly, it points a finger: When you were in your village, somewhere in West Africa, you allowed yourself to be colonized and enslaved. You failed to protect your mothers, your daughters, your wives. You let yourself be brought across the ocean in shackles, and then when they took you out of the ships and sold you to a white man and told you to work in the fields, you picked up the hoe and you worked. Not at first, perhaps, but in time, in good order. There would have been no point in fighting, you surely would have lost, you might well have been killed—but still, why didn't you try? A few ran away to freedom, but of course it was dangerous and most who ran were caught, and then beaten or hobbled or hung—but still, why didn't you try? Are you, then, less than a man? Cruel history accuses and judges both slaver and slave.

That's manifestly unjust, since obviously a slave isn't responsible for his own slavery. It's like the old joke about how many psychiatrists it takes to change a lightbulb. Answer: None; the lightbulb really has to want to change itself. Did the slave, too, have to really want to free himself? He wasn't the one who created, enforced, and perpetuated the institution of slavery. He bore no responsibility for the situation—except, perhaps, in the dark night of his own soul, when he might have wondered if he had done all that a man, a real man, should do.

I'm not a believer in any hereditary theory in which psychological wounds automatically get passed down through the centuries, like some kind of stigmata of the mind. But I do think that if the circumstances are conducive, the agony of one generation can echo in the next, and the next, and the next—ever more faintly, perhaps, but still with the amplitudes and frequencies of the original. For more than a century since emancipation, African-American men have faced alternatives that looked much like those that faced the slave men: You can work in a system that intends to make good use of your labor and your genius and your strength, and then perhaps pat you on the back, but not really let you participate as a partner in the enterprise, or you can rebel and throw wrenches into the machine.

I believe it's no exaggeration to say that each of those im-
pulses is alive in each of us, alive and vital, neither one very far
from the surface, either one capable of breaking out at any moment. I don't mean that there's actual violence in each of us, just
the violent impulse, not necessarily acted on, not necessarily even
acknowledged, but there—the impulse, the wish, to slit the throat
of the man with the whip and then run for the hills, following the
darkened trails toward the North Star and blessed freedom.

That's an awful lot of ballast, and being a black man in
America isn't an easy thing. I suppose it really isn't easy being
anything in America these days. But I don't know how it feels to
be, say, a fifty-year-old white man and see minorities just a few
years out of graduate school leapfrogging past you to get the
plum jobs you've long wanted, minorities who may objectively
be more qualified, or may not, who may be smarter, or may not,
but in any event should have had to wait their turn, just like you
did. I don't know how it feels to be a white woman who knows
she's brighter and more capable than anyone else in the office,
but whose career plans will suffer irretrievably if she has a child.
I don't know how it feels to be a Chinese-American high school
senior who has dedicated his whole life to his studies, and as a
reward gets to read rejection letters from colleges that already
have more than enough yellows and not nearly enough browns
and blacks.

What I do know is the chill up the spine that black men in
America always, always feel when they're being pulled over by a
policeman for any reason. I know the humiliation of standing in
the street for five minutes, fifteen minutes, a half-hour, trying to
hail a taxi, being ignored by empty cab after empty cab whose
drivers think that I'm going to the wrong side of town, or that I
might not tip them properly, or that I might even mean them bod-

ily harm. I know the way that people who first encounter me on the phone, and thus have no idea what I look like, do a little double take, a mental adjustment, when I meet them face-to-face. I am a professional in my forties who doesn't dress like a hip-hopper or a thug, and yet I know the sound of car doors locking when they pull up to a stoplight where I'm waiting to walk across the street. These are all little things, each of them inconsequential. Yet they and a thousand other little things add up to something bigger, something much harder to deal with.

Was this what race was all about? Was it about carrying three-hundred-year-old baggage around on my back all the time? Was it, after all this time, still about black professionals feeling caught between a black world and a white world? Was it about worrying whether my way of being an African American was the right way, or at least a way that I could be comfortable with? Was it about living with subliminal tension so insidious and powerful that every once in a while I just exploded like a lunatic and sat there vibrating until my wife could talk me back down?

I knew, long before I ever set foot in Brazil, that there was violence in me, mild-mannered me, that there was bitterness inside me, and anger, and a certain capacity for pure rage. It was bottled, capped, plugged; it let off steam from time to time; it never really exploded into anything beyond shouting or sulking, but it was there.

And yet somehow Brazil took the anger out. Which brings me back to that sidewalk in São Paulo.

In America I'd have felt an obligation to insist on my right-of-way. After all, there was a time, not all that long ago, when black people in the South—and even in much of the rest of the country—were expected to step aside as a matter of course and let whites pass. That day was long gone, but sometimes it seemed to me that I had both the right and the duty to reinforce the point. All of which led to any number of unnecessary collisions and a fair amount of self-induced stress over something that didn't even rise to the level of triviality.

In Brazil this whole context was missing. Even if I didn't know everything I needed to know about the country's history or its attitudes toward race, I sensed the difference in the way people interacted. When I walked down the sidewalk in Rio or São Paulo or anywhere else in the country, I knew that for once I didn't have to insist on what I was owed at all costs. I had another option, one that was perfectly acceptable: I could just step aside.

When I was standing in line, waiting for a beachside vendor to sell me a bottle of beer, and a white couple jumped the queue, I didn't have to make a scene — I could just shrug and wait. When a white passerby or merchant or waiter gave me a look that seemed aggressive, I didn't have to stare him down — I could just look away. I could accept life in this laid-back way because it was evident that black Brazilians were equally laid-back in their casual encounters with whites. The imperative to insist simply wasn't there.

I knew one black Brazilian man who, in the context of a society where most black people don't think of themselves as black, was positively militant compared to his compatriots on the subject of race. He seemed to have a good historical sense of Brazilian slavery, a keen sense of race consciousness, and a real attitude about demanding his place in a society that had excluded him and his kind for too long. He was very dark-skinned, unambiguously black, and proud of it.

Once, in a small town, when he and I went into a little store to ask directions, the white proprietor decided to behave like a jerk, claiming not to have understood the address and pretending not to know where it was. This was an obvious lie: The town was so small that everybody knew everybody else, and there were so few streets that it was impossible to get them confused.

In the States, in that situation, I'd have looked at my friend and we'd have exchanged a confirmational glance, as if to say to each other, "Okay, we know the score, we know what's going on. Two black men here, one white man there, he's blowing us off. Screw him." But when I looked at my Brazilian friend, I got nothing back. There was no conspiracy in his eyes, and while he was plainly annoyed at being jerked around, there was none of the specific kind of anger that I'd expected to see, the kind that had to do with race.

It was no big thing, really, just a passing moment, but it told me a lot. I remember it vividly, because it was a moment in which I felt cheated somehow. At the time we were in the heart of black Brazil, having spent hours talking about race and culture, having just eaten lunch at a restaurant whose walls were covered with local carvings that could have been done in Ghana or Benin, a setting in which I was about as fired up with race consciousness as I could ever get, and filled with an anger that went all the way back to the slave ships. Yet from the black people around me I saw no willingness to feel racial anger and then to use that anger to bring us closer together.

It's hard to describe meaningfully the absence of something, but the absence of racial anger was something I noticed immediately in Brazil, a vibe I picked up on my early visits. It was evident in the dancing crowd at the Salgueiro samba school, among the multitudes on the beaches, in everyday interactions between blacks and whites in offices and hotel lobbies and restaurants. The racial tension that you so often saw in mixed encounters in America simply didn't seem to exist.

Once, for a story we were working on, Mac Margolis took me to a favela, or slum, called Jacarezinho—"Little Cayman"—where the local drug trade was controlled by a gangster nicknamed Half-Kilo. You don't just wander into these slums without a contact; ours was a man who worked as a messenger at the house where Mac and the other expatriate journalists had their offices. Armed with a few introductions, we made our way through the city—to a part of it that looked nothing at all like the postcard beaches—and finally found ourselves cruising slowly through Jacarezinho's narrow main drag. The place was poor and makeshift, but at the same time full of life and color, and it was hard to imagine that at night the street often rang with gunfire.

We arrived at the address we had been given, and our host—a brown-skinned man in his thirties—took us up to the rooftop of his house. It was a substantial place, four stories high, but far from opulent, made almost entirely of cinderblock and concrete. Like almost all the other houses in this improvised settlement, it was unfinished, the roof a forest of steel reinforcing rods sticking out of stubby posts—at some point, when there was enough money, he planned to add a fourth floor.

Mac and I sat there for hours on that roof, looking out over the street life of Jacarezinho, drinking beer with a half-dozen of our host's friends who spent the evening telling us about their lives, their fears, and their dreams. It was a fascinating introduction to everyday life in urban Brazil, and it touched a familiar chord: I'd participated in just that sort of scene as a reporter visiting housing projects in America. But there was a difference. In America, the project dwellers I'd talked to had all been black, and they'd talked about their problems in terms of race. In Brazil, the slum dwellers were mostly black, and race wasn't mentioned, not once. These people had a lot to be angry about, but being black in a society where the rich and powerful were all white — which indeed was the case — didn't figure on their list of complaints. If anything, these men seemed happy and optimistic. I wondered whether this didn't have something to do with the absence of racial anger that I perceived. Anger took so much out of a person, ended up being such a drain on one's resources. I remembered the spent, bitter people I'd interviewed in Hunters Point or Anacostia or the Cass Corridor or other slums in America. These people in Jacarezinho were much poorer, they were every bit as hassled by the police and neglected by officialdom and marginalized by a modern economy that refused to wait for them to catch up, but they didn't see any of this circumstance in racial terms. They didn't feel that the sum total of their oppression resulted from their being black. To me, in many ways, they seemed much happier.

HAPPINESS, I discovered, can be contagious.

One time in Rio I decided to visit a couple of American colleagues — Sam Dillon and Julia Preston — who lived not far from where Mac had his office. I arrived at the appointed hour, walked up to the door of their apartment building, and rang the bell. I could see the doorman inside, but for some reason he didn't just buzz me in. Instead, he kept motioning for me to go around to the right, through the carport.

He met me at the rear entrance and looked me over, somewhat warily. When I explained that I'd come to visit my friends, the American journalists who lived in the big apartment on the top floor, he politely and efficiently showed me in. I thought nothing of it.

It wasn't until much later, after I'd spent a pleasant evening with Sam and Julia and gone back to my hotel, that I realized what had happened. The doorman, seeing a brown-skinned, nappy-headed man petition for entry, had shown me around to the service entrance. Whatever ambiguity there might have been about the proper terminology for my race, as far as he was concerned I was dark enough and African enough to be placed well toward the bottom of the racial hierarchy. Moreover, I was wearing a T-shirt, slacks, and tennis shoes, normal Rio de Janeiro garb, nothing to make me look like anything but a *carioca*. He doubtless assumed I must have been a deliveryman, a tradesman of some sort, maybe a messenger. Maybe even, in a worst case scenario, an armed robber.

But then I spoke, and once he heard my accent and realized I was a foreigner, he assigned me a new, higher racial category. Accordingly, I received the treatment that that higher category deserved.

The incident stuck in my mind because the doorman himself was unambiguously black, a good deal darker than me.

It took me a long time to process that encounter, to begin to figure out what had happened. A black man, seeing another black man approach, had automatically sent him to the tradesmen's entrance. All right, that much could have happened in Jim Crow America. But he'd done it without a nod, or a wink, or any acknowledgment of shared heritage, shared condition. There was no acknowledgment that while this was perhaps necessary — because that was what was expected of him to keep his job, because that was just the way things were — it was still wrong. Nor had he been particularly aggressive about it, as a certain stratum of self-hating Negroes had been during the Jim Crow years. He hadn't taken any pleasure or any sense of superiority from it, at least that I could detect; he had just done what he was expected to do. Meanwhile, I had been complicit in the scenario because I had failed to react with any sort of outrage. After having spent so much time in Brazil, I realized that my racism sensor had been re-calibrated, or maybe just turned off.

Later, I started playing a game with myself. When I was con-ducting interviews in Brazil, I began routinely asking black peo-ple—dark-skinned people, I mean, since many of them didn't think of themselves as black—if they'd ever been sent to the back entrance or the service elevator when they were calling on white acquaintances. Almost all said they had. The interesting thing was that most were willing to chalk it up to the way they'd been dressed or the way they'd acted, not exclusively to the color of their skin. Almost none were angry about it. Many people, when I told them of my own experience, simply explained it as a door-man displaying reasonable caution at the approach of a man he'd never seen before in a crime-ridden city where it was impossible to be too careful.

At first, when I talked to these black people who didn't think they were black, I wondered if I should be angry for them. But then my own anger began to subside, certainly not because I thought the slights less serious, or more acceptable, but because the people I met in Brazil generally were so happy. I have read in some science magazine that there are some sufferers of chronic pain who through some new miracle drug or therapy are cured of their suffering, and then find that they *miss* the pain, that they ac-tually regret its absence. I felt as if I, too, were longing for a pain that had miraculously vanished. Who needed pain? Who needed to feel eaten up by suspicion, by mistrust, by anger, by all these corrosive feelings that might not even be called for? What was wrong with trusting that people weren't going to treat me badly because of the color of my skin?

And anyway, maybe the guard *was* just being careful.

Chapter 6

Colors

WHAT BRAZIL REALLY MADE ME THINK ABOUT WAS COLOR. I HAD thought, all my life, that I knew what skin color meant, which was, specifically, that it didn't mean anything at all except as a broad indicator of the more important category called race. In Brazil, though, it was race that meant very little and color that seemed to mean everything.

Two stories:

Some time in late 1978 or early 1979, a few months after Avis and I had gotten married and while we were still living in San Francisco, my father called to remind me that he had a cousin who lived not far from where we did, my "Aunt" Sarah, whom I'd never met. I was young and independent, and in a sense I suppose one of my reasons for being in San Francisco in the first place was to be as far away as possible from the embrace of family and the familiar. In four years of living in the Bay Area, I hadn't even dropped by Aunt Sarah's house to say hello. But now Avis and I were newlyweds, and in a family mood—she wanted to know more about mine, I wanted to know more about hers—and so one afternoon we tooled down to Daly City for a visit.

The address was in a tidy, middle-class neighborhood of stucco houses with flat roofs, a quiet place that looked as if it hadn't changed since the 1950s. I rang the bell, the door opened, and there stood a short, stout, handsome woman of advancing years, who in every particular of hair, skin, and eye looked white—not café au lait, not mulatto, just plain old white. She gave me a big hug and ushered us in.

Sarah seemed delighted to see us. As we talked in the living room, which had better light than the shadowy doorway, I could see that her skin had a slight undertone of beige, with no hint of pink. It was an effect so subtle that it could have been achieved with makeup alone, but it was there—and it was the only possible indication that she was anything but pure Caucasian.

Then, a few minutes later, from somewhere deep in the house emerged her grown son, another cousin I'd never met. I'm afraid I was impolite; I was raised to know that it's rude to stare, but that's what I did.

If Sarah was perhaps just barely identifiable as potentially, maybe, just possibly a person of color, her son betrayed no trace, gave not the slightest hint. With his straight sandy brown hair and his ruddy complexion he was, simply, white.

Except when he talked. What came out of his mouth wasn't quite black English, but close. His speech was broad and vaguely southern—although it didn't really sound as if he'd ever lived in the South—and somewhat relaxed in its grammar and cadence. He dropped final g's and elided inconvenient syllables remorselessly. With my eyes closed I'd have been absolutely sure that this was a black man.

We spent a few pleasant hours talking about relatives I'd never met, and then Avis and I left. I was stunned. As Avis pointed out, I really shouldn't have been so surprised. I knew full well that throughout my family history, as throughout the family histories of most African Americans, white ancestors were sprinkled here and there. My father's skin, for example, is a bit darker than mine, but he has hazel-colored eyes, a legacy of genes that doubtless arose far from the mother continent. Before meeting any distant relative for the first time, I'd never been able to make a reliable assumption about whether he'd be light-skinned or dark-skinned; there was ample precedent for both conditions, on both sides of my family. But in this case the contrast was so great that it made me do something I don't usually do, something we're trained not to do.

It made me take notice of color.

Flash forward a dozen years or so to Brazil. In the northeast I met a woman named Dora Dias who was active in the nascent black consciousness movement. She was coppery brown, with curly black hair, and I remember that she smiled and chain-smoked while she described for me, in more or less formulaic "movement" language, the work she did. She ran a school, which had hundreds of students and seemed to be doing good and necessary work. Progress was being made. Still, one of the hardest things she encountered was trying to get people to identify themselves as black. There were too few black officials, she said, and many of the black officials didn't call themselves black, even though anybody could see that they were.

I asked about her personal experience of race: What was it like to be black in her country?

She thought for a minute, lit another cigarette, and told a story.

Dora had two children, both of them much lighter-skinned than she is. "You know how it is—you never know how they'll come out. It's probably the same with you, in your family. Anything is possible. Their father is lighter than I am. Anyhow, I'm black. That's what it says on my birth certificate, and on their father's too. But on both my children's birth certificates, it says that they're white. My own children, the children of a black woman, and the society considers them white."

One day, when her children were quite young, she was out walking with them. They were about to cross a busy street when the younger one began to cry and the older one became rambunctious. She snatched them rudely, as a frustrated young mother will do, and they bawled even louder, as young kids will do, and what had begun as a little episode quickly escalated into a real scene. When she had finally wrestled them across the street she was shocked to see a policeman running toward her full tilt. The cop grabbed her, demanded that she identify herself, and asked where she had gotten these children. Gradually it emerged that he believed he had apprehended a black woman in the act of kidnapping two white children for ransom. Only when the frightened kids called her "Mae!"—"Mommy!"—did he relent.

Those were the extremes of the experience of color: being shocked to see it at all, and being unable to see anything else. And I'd just gone from the domain of one to the domain of the other.

TO MY EYES, at least initially, the most striking thing about skin color in Brazil was how many colors there were. Granted, at first I was looking through an American filter that essentially polarized every shade into either black or white. By triangulating features, hair texture, and skin tone, I was able to put most of the people I saw on the streets of Salvador or Rio or even São Paulo into the broad American category "people of color," with most of that fraction managing to fit into the American racial group called "black." But I soon came to see that this was an oversimplification, if only because the variety of skin tones was so rich and so subtle—and so evenly distributed.

Here's another way to put it: Assign every individual's skin tone a number—the darker the skin, the higher the number—and then plot these numbers on a graph. In the United States, assuming you were just dealing with blacks and whites, you'd have one distinct cluster at the bottom end, for whites, and then another distinct cluster at the top end, for blacks. The white cluster would be relatively compact. The black cluster would be much more diffuse, since it would have a wider range of skin tones to take into account, but it would still be distinct as a cluster, and it would have a center, a dense concentration somewhere around medium brown, that in statistical terms would represent the "mode" for black Americans, or the largest number of individuals.

If you plotted that same graph in Brazil, the result would be quite different. There would still be a cluster of whites, but it would be more diffuse, representing a somewhat wider color range. And the black Brazilians wouldn't really form a cluster at all. Rather, they would be plotted into a relatively smooth distribution, all the way from coal to cream, stretching from the darkest "after midnight" shades right up to the edge of the white cluster, and without a discernible concentration representing the largest number of individuals—without a mode. You'd be much less able to say what an "average" or "representative" black Brazilian looked like.

If you factored in hair texture, facial features, body type, and other "racial" identifiers, the contrast would be heightened: two fairly defined groups in the United States, more of a spectrum in Brazil.

What I saw in Brazil was a continuum in which some people were clearly white, some were clearly black, and everyone else was either blacker or whiter—but only blacker or whiter in relation to everyone else. Many individuals fit into that nether region where there was no absolute racial identity, just broad categories—light-skinned, mulatto, brownish—that had no boundaries that were fully agreed upon. In other words, you had fairly wide latitude to be whatever you wanted to be.

Once I understood this, I saw that it went a long way toward explaining why there was so little overt racial fear and loathing in Brazil among individuals. Just whom are you supposed to fear and loathe? Whom do you include in the "us" of the scenario "us versus them"? Where do you draw the line?

In a sense it was like a glimpse into a possible—and possibly glorious—American future. Isn't America becoming more like Brazil? Aren't there more interracial marriages? Isn't there a wave of immigrants from the rest of the Americas, the immigrants themselves already mixed-race, now further mixing with white Americans and black Americans? Aren't we filling the kindergartens with beige and tan children who will grow up with a very different, and perhaps more enlightened, idea of what race is and can be and should be?

The thing that so excited me about the future I saw in Brazil was the absence of solid walls. The categories I'd grown up with that were so much a part of my being—the categories black and white—just tended to melt away in Brazil. They didn't matter in the same way. I felt liberated from them, liberated to the point of exhilaration. But if race was less distinct and less categorical than in America, and color was more important, then I felt I needed to try to understand what color meant in Brazil. So I looked around, trying to dampen my emotional response, my naked enthusiasm. And I kept coming back to a piece of doggerel I'd learned as a child in Orangeburg, half a world away:

"If you're white, all right. If you're brown, stick around. But if you're black, get back."

That clearly seemed to be the color scheme, in a process that didn't quite qualify as overt discrimination—certainly not racial discrimination as we know it, since race was so indeterminate—but that nonetheless seemed to have real power.

It was hard to get at, except impressionistically. I remember interviewing a woman at the beach for a political story I was writing, a dark-skinned woman with clearly African hair and features, and her responding to one question by saying, "I don't really know, you should ask my boyfriend. He's the light-skinned guy over there playing volleyball." It wasn't what she said, since light-skinned was an accurate description of her man, but the way she said it—with a kind of smugness and pride.

I asked Mac Margolis about it later. "It's a status thing for a lot of women, to have a light-skinned boyfriend," he told me.

Then there were the images I'd see on billboards or in magazine ads. There were so many blonde, blue-eyed models selling milk or televisions that it might as well have been Sweden. Black people were few, far between, and generally speaking not very black. The pecking order, from light at the top to dark at the bottom, was becoming obvious.

If you're black, get back.

For some black Americans, especially in the old-line southern cities like Charleston and Atlanta and New Orleans, skin color was once an attribute that determined who was able to enter polite black society and who not, who was eligible to marry into certain leading families and who not, who was assumed to be a promising candidate for higher education, special attention, future prominence—and who not. To some extent, American Negroes bought into the lighter-is-righter prejudice of the larger society. The black leadership in America, for longer that we like to admit, was largely light-skinned; and to a greater extent than we like to admit, African Americans at the top of our stubby socioeconomic pyramid historically segregated themselves by color. By the time I was growing up, in the late fifties and early sixties, that kind of overt color prejudice was almost gone—almost, but not quite. There was a visible legacy, in the straight hair and light skin of the members of socially and politically prominent black families in Washington, New York, Philadelphia, and other major cities—in the Percy Suttons and Adam Clayton Powells and Roy Wilkinses of the world.

As for my own family, this was really no issue. For one thing, we were all different colors, from dark to light. For another, nobody really cared about achieving any kind of prominence in "society," such as it was. My parents weren't big party-goers, and anyway black Orangeburg was more of a meritocracy, based as it was on education and accomplishment.

But there were still echoes and reminders of this old, color-conscious way of thinking, even in a home like mine. The black-oriented magazines that came to our house, *Ebony* and *Jet*, were full of ads for "miracle" creams that would lighten your skin. Even more numerous were the magazines' big, glossy ads for every imaginable poultice or device that plausibly or implausibly claimed to make kinky hair straight. African Americans were spending eons of time and Fort Knoxes of money in an endless attempt to turn hair that God intended to be coarse and kinky into hair that would blow in the wind, like the hair of white models in commercials for products like Breck and Alberto VO$_5$, hair that bounced, according to the television commercials, with an ineffable quality called "body."

I used to watch those commercials with a child's naive fascination, wondering what in the world "body" might be, and wondering how any hair could conceivably have more of it than black people's hair.

My family had a healthy sense of racial awareness, with no apparent hang-ups or identity crises. Yet my mother, grandmother, and great-aunt would go religiously to the hairdresser's to have powerful chemicals applied to their scalps, over and over again, until finally the defeated hair curled and poufed and lay down in abject submission. Then they would come home and do even worse to my sister Ellen, poor Ellen, forcing her to sit perfectly still on a stool in the kitchen for what seemed like hours while they went at her head with iron pressing combs. These were fearsome implements that would have done Torquemada proud, heated on the stove to a temperature more suitable for branding than grooming. I'd watch this process, transfixed and a little frightened, worrying that if Ellen moved a muscle she'd be seared like a prized heifer. I still remember the sweetish smell of scorched hair.

The women in my family, when I was growing up, still talked of "good" hair, and whenever they pointed out an example to admire it was long, soft, and straight. When they indicated girls they thought especially pretty, they were usually endowed with both "good" hair and light-colored skin. The irony was that the women in our house weren't particularly light-skinned themselves, not nearly as light as the "pretty" girls they pointed out. It was as if they didn't quite trust their own great beauty. My guess is that absolutely none of this was done or said consciously. They'd somehow absorbed an implicit value system, probably from the adult women who'd lived in the house when *they* were growing up, and certainly from the images of black "beauty" they saw in magazines, in which to be "beautiful" was to look white, and they were unconsciously passing it on.

The vestigial color prejudice in the United States that managed to survive the realization that black is beautiful is never, ever discussed. That's doubtless because of its traumatic, divisive, reprehensible origin. In the days of slavery, as everyone knows, light-skinned slaves were almost always the offspring of black slave mothers and white slave-owning fathers. When they grew up these mulatto slaves, blood kin to the lord of the manor, got the more desirable and less strenuous "house" jobs, while the darker lumpen worked the "field" jobs. The "house niggers" often had advantages the "field niggers" could never have, like learning to read and write; they were better fed and better sheltered, which meant they were healthier. Because of all this, they were more prepared, when emancipation came, to make their ways in the world.

Perhaps most important of all, they were believed by other black people to be less hated by whites. I say "believed" because they really weren't: The Jim Crow laws that were passed in the wake of Reconstruction applied to them just as to everyone else, perhaps to their surprise and disappointment. But the assumption was that somehow they were deemed less unacceptable, that somehow they would always get a better deal from the white world.

I didn't know enough yet to begin to understand all the subtleties of how race and skin tone intersected in Brazil, but the outlines had already become clear. Hair mattered, features mattered, but what mattered most of all was color—and lighter was better. It was apparent that in Brazil, as a general rule, white—or, at least, light—indeed made right. That was the same as in America. But there were important differences.

In colonial Brazil, a fully developed plantation society to rival the American Deep South, miscegenation was accepted more or less openly as a fact of life. I'm not quite sure why this was the case, why the level of acceptance differed so much from that in the North American colonies. Perhaps the Portuguese were just more Latin and less puritanical about sex in general than their Anglo-Saxon counterparts. Whatever the reason, black-white liaisons are acknowledged to have been extremely common in early Brazil, historians agree. Even in the earliest days of Brazilian plantation slavery, the mulatto—the half-breed—was seen as distinct from either black or white, almost as a new race.

Later, miscegenation was even encouraged by some Brazilian social theorists as a way of eliminating, or at least closing, the wide racial gap that existed after emancipation. The idea was that intermarriage would eventually "whiten" the nation, evening out racial differences by blurring the lines between the races. This blurring eventually became part and parcel of the Brazilian national myth. Legislators enacted laws making racial discrimination illegal, and then convinced themselves, and the rest of the nation, that they had banished this evil forever. The country's leading men of letters—from sociologist Gilberto Freyre, who proclaimed his nation a "racial democracy," to novelist Jorge Amado, whose books celebrate Brazil's racial mix—have all traditionally bought into the idea of racial mixing as good rather than bad, a major element in the Brazilian "genius" for life and fun and happiness.

In the American South, by contrast, despite the many liaisons between white masters and black slaves that produced generations of mulatto children—that indeed produced me, my wife, my parents, and the overwhelming majority of African Americans, since most of us have at least some white blood—miscegenation was officially taboo. The offspring of these liaisons may have been allowed to do softer "house" work on the plantations rather than "field" work, they may even been taught to read and write, but they were still unambiguously black.

After the Civil War, as soon as southern whites escaped the strictures imposed by Reconstruction, the first thing they did was enact laws designed to keep blacks and whites separate. There remained a deep-seated fear of intimacy between blacks and whites, especially between black men and white women. The classic pretext for a Mississippi lynching was a wicked leer or a lewd remark allegedly inflicted by a predatory black man upon the chaste and pristine bosom of white southern womanhood. Sexual congress between a black man and a white woman in the South was, for the man, a capital offense.

Yet love, or lust, found a way. And the proof is all around us, live and in living color—if we can bring ourselves to notice.

It's amazing, when you think about it, what cultural conditioning can do to a society's collective eyesight. We immediately register the minute color distinction between a curly-haired, olive-skinned man whose ancestry is Greek, for example, and a curly-haired, olive-skinned man whose ancestry is African, and yet when a parchment-colored African-American man stands in vivid contrast next to his African-American buddy the color of dark chocolate, we aren't supposed to notice any distinction at all.

I have a hunch, though, that maybe in America we really do notice color, at least on some basic level. But since we can't talk about it we leave it inside, raw and unprocessed, where it poisons the way we look at one another without our even knowing it.

It's strange dichotomy. On the one hand, most black families in America, like my own, are at least to some extent multicolored, some almost kaleidoscopically. The color gap between, say, my aunt Flora and my uncle Harry was not quite as great as the gap between porcelain and obsidian, but fairly close. On the other hand, among African Americans there has always been a light-dark dynamic that at various times roughly reflected other divisions, like house-field, educated-uneducated, affluent-impoverished, urban-rural. Never was there an absolute distinction, or even enough of a relative distinction to call into question the obvious truth that all black people — black by the one-drop rule — were essentially in the same boat. But there was a correlation, one that has greatly weakened over time.

If you wanted a picture of the dichotomy you could look back at the famous philosophical debate between Booker T. Washington and W. E. B. Du Bois: Washington, in essence representing the black workingman, arguing for vocational training and against an immediate attempt by black people to claim full participation in the white world; Du Bois, celebrating the "talented tenth" of the African-American population, arguing for higher education and a campaign to push wide open all the closed doors. Both men brilliant: Washington, kinky-haired; Du Bois, straight-haired; Washington, coffee-dark; Du Bois, caramel-light.

When I was growing up I heard both of these men described in reverent terms. I knew little or nothing of their disagreement on the future of the race, and probably wouldn't have fully understood it. I did have ideas, or rather impressions, of color, but they were a child's impressions, honest but unsubtle and often wrong.

I noticed that Negroes—we were not yet black—came in all colors. I remember being confused that some families were so light-skinned and light-haired that they looked for all intents and purposes like white people. But of course they weren't, because they lived on the Negro side of town and went to Negro churches and had Negro friends. Among the people my family associated with, there was not much of a color pattern. But from reading *Ebony* and *Jet* I was aware that there was a society-conscious Negro upper crust, and I had the vague impression that these people, who mostly lived in places like Washington and Atlanta, were light-skinned.

On the other side of the spectrum there were various shades of Negro poverty: Sunnyside, with its overcrowded little tin-roofed shacks on brick-pillar stilts; little hamlets out in the country, rural areas down lonesome roads with their ramshackle houses with linoleum-floored living rooms, ancient pot-bellied stoves and the constant smell of hog manure. The people who lived in these shacks, both in the city and on the farm, tended to be very dark.

This wasn't anything that I ever concentrated on, or read any significance into, or otherwise dealt with except to let it make a visual impression, just like everything else that passed before my young eyes. I wouldn't have known how to raise the issue with anyone—I wouldn't have even thought there was an issue to be raised. That was just the way things were.

I do have mental snapshots: Gloria Washington was about my age, maybe a little bit older. Her family lived in a big house out on U.S. 601. Glo-Glo was so light-skinned that I thought there was essentially no difference between her skin color and that of white people, although I knew the Washingtons were Negroes. The family owned a small poultry farm; I remember going out there to see the chickens and to see the building where they inspected, sorted, and packaged the eggs. I remember vast long conveyors, not moving belts but spinning metal rollers, designed so the eggs could glide down to be candled and crated without breaking.

Mrs. Lovely Mae White, my third-grade and fourth-grade teacher, had dark brown skin; she was the darkest of the four teachers who ruled Felton's eight grades. It was a third-grader's idea of supreme irony that someone named Mrs. White would in fact be so brown.

Rev. Hank McCollum, the pastor at Trinity Church, was very dark and very distinguished, ramrod tall, and spoke with a voice full of gravel and import, a voice like I imagined the voice of Moses. His successor, Rev. James Curry, was a bit lighter, kind of a milk chocolate brown, with a deeper voice that resounded through the sanctuary. Mr. Earl Middleton, who used to cut my hair and later went on to hold a seat in the state legislature, had skin more in the range of semisweet chocolate.

When I was in school at Felton, the girls who were generally considered pretty were medium-to light-skinned, with long wavy hair—"good" hair. Girls with coarse hair had to endure having it pressed and then secured with barrettes or bands. It looked the way it was supposed to look at the beginning of the day, but by the time recess was over the hair was beginning to escape in wisps that stood up on the girls' heads like quills. Debbie Smith, who was butternut colored, had hair that did this. So did Belinda Davis, who was a velvety brown.

The principal at Felton for most of my time there was Mrs. Maxine Crawford, my torment and my greatest inspiration. She was one of the Sulton clan, one of the most prominent black families in town, and had known my family all her life. Whenever I misbehaved in school it was a simple matter of Mrs. Crawford calling her childhood friend Louisa—my mother—to ensure that I got punished at home as well as at school. Like all the Sultons, she was light-skinned with straight hair. When I was in seventh grade, the old four-room Felton schoolhouse was replaced with a new modern facility, a sprawling building that had plenty of space but little character. The new principal was a Mrs. Roberts, who was heavy and very dark.

It feels odd to look back at these faces and see them in true color. It's easier, and perhaps more natural, to see them in racial color, as black people in the all-black world of my childhood. To see them as light or dark, as coffee or café au lait, I have to think back and call up the image. It's not that the information isn't there, it's just that it's somehow incompletely processed. In this decidedly uncolorblind world this is one sense in which we *are* colorblind. It feels wrong, for some reason, to look at color and notice it and record it and play it back in this fashion—sinfully wrong, an unnatural act.

I look at my own arms and my own legs, I look at my own face in the mirror, and I see a black man of light-to-medium complexion. It's easier for me to write about the color of people who are lighter-skinned than me, than it is to write about those who are darker. I have absolutely no problem writing about the Sultons or the Washingtons as light-skinned families, but it's hard for me to write the truthful statement that when I recall the slum dwellings of Sunnyside I see dark-skinned people and hardly any others. It's hard because I'm afraid of being misunderstood. I'm afraid it will look as if I'm trying to set myself up as superior, as if I'm trying to correlate dark skin with poverty and all its ills. I'm afraid, in short, that it will look like I'm acting like I've always accused unenlightened white people of acting, seeing the world through discriminating eyes that equate light with good and dark with bad.

BUT THEN WHAT did any of this really amount to, except taking notice of the obvious? The truth is that some people have lighter skin than others and some people have darker skin than others, even within what we think of as racial groups. What could be wrong with acknowledging the simple truth?

Brazil compelled that acknowledgment, in a way that I found refreshing and hopeful. The analogy I kept thinking of was a child who is convinced that there are monsters lurking in his closet. What any parent does is open the closet door, turn on the light, and demonstrate that there's nothing monstrous inside at all. Color was a door that we didn't open in America because we *knew* there were all sorts of monsters in there. But here was a society where people dealt with skin color as a fact of daily life, where they kept the closet door open and somehow they weren't eaten alive. What they did with color—use it to help define a social pecking order—was hardly admirable, but at the same time it didn't seem so bad to me, primarily because it was so fluid and so forgiving. I was light in some contexts and dark in others, and that very uncertainty seemed to rob the pecking order of its seriousness and make it almost a game.

It's not a very great leap to wonder whether America couldn't be more like this, whether, in fact, our country wouldn't inevitably become more like Brazil whether we want it to or not. The distribution along the American color spectrum is beginning to even out, just a bit. Isn't that where we are headed, to a situation where race is less useful as a descriptive concept than the simple evidence of color?

If so, it seemed to me that we had little to fear, that, in fact, we had much to anticipate, even to celebrate. Once we could get past the barrier of admitting that some people had darker skin than others then there was no reason why that distinction wouldn't eventually become a normal distinction like any other. We manage to deal, for example, with our society's clear bias toward tall people; we've reduced it to something that exists, but has no real meaning, that frames no real issue. Some people are tall and some are short; we recognize it, and we get over it. Why couldn't we do the same with color? And if we could do that, then why did we need this difficult, wrenching concept called race at all?

We could turn our backs on it. We could embrace the raceless future that was sure to come.

Chapter 7

The Future That Never Came

BRASÍLIA LOOKS LIKE SOMETHING OUT OF THE JETSONS; IT LOOKS like the place where we all were supposed to live, in the future that never came.

The city, Brazil's bizarre capital, was carved out of the red earth of a high interior plateau. It's laid out in the shape of a modern jetliner, with government ministries along the fuselage, the twin towers housing the Brazilian congress in the nose, and businesses and apartments occupying the swept-back wings. It is one of the oddest urban places on earth, with everyone living in identical International-style, glass-and-concrete apartment blocks, grouped in identical sectors with "names" like 301-S. There is no relationship between the land and the city imposed upon it; the idea, when the place was built from scratch in the late 1950s, was that the automobile and the bus were to be the prescribed modes of transportation of the future, meaning that people would drive from home to office to recreational facility, from environment to environment to environment, without actually having anything to do with the land at all. The streets are all laid out with cloverleafs and overpasses instead of conventional intersections, and in the whole city there are practically no sidewalks. Drunks must have an interesting time finding their way home.

Brasília, of all places, was the city in Brazil that I first visited in my imagination. Not exotic Rio, not dynamic São Paulo, not historic Salvador, but weird, sterile, characterless Brasília. It was the place that first connected with me, long before I ever dreamed I'd actually get to that part of the world.

So it's only fitting, I suppose, that Brasília is the place where my sense of what race really meant in Brazil, and thus my sense of what race really meant to me, began to change—the place where I began to fall out of love. Brazil jilted me in Brasília, and it took me a long time to forgive her.

MY MIND'S EYE first saw Brasília when I was in fourth grade.

Sitting there in Lovely Mae White's class at Felton one day, I picked up the latest *Weekly Reader* and learned of the new, ultramodern Brazilian capital. I'm not entirely sure I knew quite where Brazil was at the time, and I don't remember what the article said. But I do remember the pictures: photographs of these amazing modern buildings, skyscrapers and office blocks and a soaring modernist cathedral like a concrete teepee. These structures weren't just scattered here and there as they would have been in any other city, but rather *arranged* just so, laid out on a vast, empty plain with nothing in between, nothing to crowd

them, nothing to distract. It was just the way I would have designed and built a city with my Lego blocks. I was captivated. I
was in thrall to Brasília.

I kept this image in my mind and in my heart for many years.
All through grade school and high school, I told anyone who
asked that I intended to become an architect. I wanted to build
environments that were stark, pure, uncompromising, and
Brasília was my template.

This plan came to a quick, merciful, and entirely justified end
just a few weeks after I'd arrived in Ann Arbor and enrolled in
the University of Michigan's School of Architecture and Design.
Of the hundred or so freshmen in Architecture 101, I was easily
the most incompetent. The world is a much safer place without
me at the drawing board.

I got the first hint when we were assigned to build a bridge,
using just balsa wood and string, that would span three feet
and support a full half-gallon can of Hi-C grape drink. The
bridge that weighed the least earned the highest grade. Mine
was bulky and asymmetrical, full of redundant parts, and so
weak that to keep it from snapping I had to insert two thick
wooden dowels that by themselves probably would have done
the job. It weighed 45 grams—a C-plus. The winner, designed
by a wraith named Rich, was a slim, graceful arch that weighed
7 grams and would have supported me. I took from this a lesson about aptitude.

Then there was the term project: building a model of a house,
any house, from an architecture magazine. I worked long and
hard on mine, and was extremely proud of it—at least until the
day came to turn it in. All the others were beautifully crafted and
landscaped, with little trees on little hillsides and little people
strolling down the little sidewalks. Mine, now that I looked at it a

bit more critically, was a lopsided box on a plain unadorned piece of white posterboard, with both the box and the board smeared with glue. I took from this a second lesson about aptitude.

Meanwhile, I had gone to work for the student newspaper, the *Michigan Daily,* and was regularly getting articles published. My teaching fellow in English had nagged me to flesh out an essay I'd written about the student killings in Orangeburg and submit it to a campus literary competition. I won first place, and, more important, I won some money. I took from this a final lesson about aptitude and transferred out of architecture a few weeks later.

But I never lost my interest in beautiful buildings, and I never lost that pristine image of Brasília. One day, I told myself over and over again, I'd go and see it for myself.

AND SO, ONE DAY, there I stood before those buildings I remembered from that *Weekly Reader.* Brasília was a bit down at the heels now—Brazil had been through some hard times—but still, as architecture, it remained strong and pure. I spent hours just wandering around with my camera, taking pictures, looking at the major buildings from different angles. Climbing up embankments and darting across highways in a city that still, after more than thirty years, was determined to live without enough sidewalks.

But of course I was there to work, not to wander. No one ever came to Brasília for any reason other than to deal with the federal government, and I had interviews booked with a number of officials. So I walked out through the rosewood-paneled lobby of my hotel, the Hotel Nacional—itself a museum of lava lamp–era decor—grabbed a cab, rocketed through some disorienting loops and turns, and ended up at one of the identical office blocks that march down the main esplanade.

I went up to the door and stepped out of Brazil, looking-glass style, into a different place, a faraway place, a place that looked more like Portugal.

What had happened to my "great black nation"? Here, in this important government building in the capital, it looked like everybody who was running the place was white. The secretaries, the functionaries, the high-ranking bureaucrats called "maharajahs," the press spokesmen, the technocrats, the paper-pushers, and the political appointees were white. There were a few black faces, but they belonged to the security guards, the janitors, and the other support staff. Here amid the fiber and sinew of the Brazilian public service, I could have been in any country in southern Europe. I felt a world away from the Brazil I'd left just outside the door.

That evening I went out into one of the city's residential neighborhoods, and I use the term loosely, to have dinner at an Italian restaurant that friends had recommended. The food was mediocre but the sociology was eye-opening: Here, too, the patrons were white, the valet parking attendants black. In fact, from the children I saw playing near the apartment buildings and the couples I saw strolling hand-in-hand, it looked as if the whole neighborhood were mostly white.

The next day I walked over to the central bus depot, which lies at the very center of the city, the point from which both the fuselage axis and the wing axis extend. Once again, I felt comfortable and at home. The bus station was Brazil—bustling, poor, full of life, mostly black. Then I went to more ministries and, once again, they were Portugal—as lily-white as a government office in Orangeburg in, say, 1962.

Later that afternoon a Canadian journalist I knew invited me to have drinks at the Canadian embassy, which on Friday evenings became a kind of expatriate "pub" for English-speaking diplomats, journalists, businessmen, and others who happened to be in town. As we sat around the pool drinking beer, I quizzed these longtimers about this bizarre city they lived in and the distinct racial pattern I was perceiving.

There was no common ground: These people, who themselves happened to be white, hadn't noticed or made much of the pattern. I certainly couldn't find anyone to share my incipient outrage. There was general agreement, though, that despite its apparent sterility, Brasília was a great place to raise children, to engage in pursuits like tennis and hiking, to live a relatively stress-free life. And there was unanimity that if I wanted to really understand Brasília and Brazil, I had to go to a place called the Valley of the Dawn.

I asked why.

They said I'd see why. Just go.

So the next day, I went.

It turned out that Brasília, which I'd always thought of as a citadel of modernity, was also something of a temple of mysticism. There were geomancers who believed the city to have been built at a point where all kinds of unseen forces somehow intersected. Many bizarre legends had built up about the place over the years, the most fanciful of which—the most ridiculous, really—was that the last Inca chieftain, fleeing from Pizarro's conquistadors in Peru, had descended the eastern slope of the Andes and somehow made his way all the way across the continent to reestablish his kingdom briefly, along with a band of followers, near the site where the Brazilian government later chose to build its capital. Another legend involved a prediction by a nineteenth-

century Italian priest that the capital of a great nation would be
built at Brasília's approximate location. Other legends held that
Brasília was a popular place for sightings of UFOs and extraterrestrials, sort of the Roswell of the southern hemisphere.

It all had something to do with the elevation, the latitude and
longitude, the prevailing winds, probably the rotation of the
galaxy and the expansion of the universe. In any event, various
cults had coalesced around the idea that there was something
privileged about the city's location, something special about the
spot.

One of the bigger cults was founded in 1959 by a woman
named Tia Neiva in a declivity not far from town called the Valley
of the Dawn. I hired a cab and went out for a look.

My driver was a black man, a committed Christian who kept
a crucifix on the dashboard and a well-thumbed Bible on the seat
next to him, and who, when I told him where I wanted to go,
promptly gave me a lecture about how all this cult stuff was sa-
tanic and how all these cultists were certainly on their way to
eternal damnation in the depths of hell.

We drove all the way out the city's eastern "wing" until the
wide avenue became a divided highway. Abruptly the city ended,
and suddenly we were driving through what looked like parkland.
This went on for miles and miles; the planners of Brasília, believing that urban sprawl would mar their work, had decreed that the
jet-shaped city would be surrounded on all sides by a wide, un-
spoiled greenbelt meant to serve the same purpose as a frame
around a work of art. It was beautiful but odd, reinforcing the notion of a city that refused in any way to be like a normal city.

Finally we turned off the main highway onto a smaller road
heading toward the Valley of the Dawn, and immediately we
plunged into a little town called Planaltina.

All at once, I understood.

It looked like just another poor, dusty, broken-down Brazilian town. Barefoot youngsters played in the streets; women trudged through their daily errands; men idled at the ubiquitous little open-air bars that served ice-cold beer and sold individual ciagarettes for a few pennies each. Everything was slightly decrepit, not quite finished, somewhat neglected. There were empty storefronts and overgrown vacant lots, garbage piles and muddy pathways. The people were of the Brazilian rainbow, from dark as coal to light as cream.

Here, in Planaltina, I had found the black people of Brasília.

I interrogated my driver, and he confirmed what I was beginning to surmise: Only the federal bureaucrats, with their good salaries that were indexed to negate the country's chronic inflation, could afford to live in those sterile but well-appointed apartment buildings downtown. On top of that, the supply of downtown housing was strictly limited for esthetic reasons, so only so much was available at any price. Working-class suburbs ordinarily would have clustered around the fringes just outside the city limits, but that area constituted the green belt and nobody at all was allowed to live there. So aside from the mid-level and higher-level bureaucrats, the diplomats, the journalists, the lobbyists, and the others who constituted the capital elite, nobody else could manage to actually live in Brasília. Everybody else — the gardeners, the maids, the security guards, the bus drivers, the janitors, the cooks — had to reside far outside the city, in satellite towns like Planaltina, and commute in by bus.

The bureaucrats, as I'd seen, were white. Most of the others, as I was seeing now, were black.

I was stunned. Here in the capital of the Brazilian "racial democracy," here in the country I was coming to love so much more than my own, I was seeing a degree of racial segregation that would have made an apartheid-era white South African blush. Planaltina and its sister cities were like townships, little Sowetos and Victorias where black folks were warehoused out of sight, out of mind. You could spend a week in the city and the only evidence you'd see of them was the area around the bus station, where they arrived in the morning and departed at night, a little eruption of Brazil in the middle of Brasília.

There always comes a day in a love affair when infatuation wears off and you open your eyes and you see the object of your affections more clearly, more critically. For me and Brazil, that was the day.

We went on to the Valley of the Dawn, which was bizarre and wonderful, kind of a mystical Disney World, or even a metaphysical Las Vegas, a grand entrance lined with giant plywood Jesuses and pyramids and Egyptian ankhs, ministers with microphones leading rituals that were supposed to be Coptic and Inca and Aztec, busloads of pilgrims from all over the country wearing long robes as they walked the streets, forming circles and praying in long-dead languages whenever the spirit moved. My driver kept pointing out groups and consigning them to the flames. "They're going to hell," he'd say. "Those over there, they're going to hell, too." Finally, he retreated to his car, and when I rejoined him at the end of the day he was deep in prayer. I couldn't tell whether it was for all these wayward souls to be saved, or for a flood or an earthquake or some other cataclysm to come quickly and wipe this nexus of blasphemy from the face of the earth.

It was just the kind of incongruous, over-the-top scene I usually loved. But for once, my mind wasn't on it.

My mind was on Planaltina. On our way back to the city I asked the driver to slow down when we passed through the little

131

town so I could get another look. We went through it at a crawl, and with every block I got angrier and more depressed. There was something ugly and wrong about what I was seeing, something that, for some reason, made me feel lost.

It was a side of Brasília that I didn't recall reading about in my *Weekly Reader.*

I WAS NO STRANGER to segregated neighborhoods, of course, having grown up in Orangeburg. The first integrated neighborhood I ever lived in was the fourth floor of West Quadrangle dormitory at the University of Michigan. It was like one of those corny war movie foxhole scenes: my roommate, Bob Fujioka, was a Hawaiian of Japanese ancestry; my best friend, Howard Straubing, was Jewish; there were WASPs and Poles and Irish Catholics and me, a sixteen-year-old stringbean from South Carolina who on some days wanted to be Huey Newton and on other days thought he was Jimi Hendrix. Throughout my college years my concept of "community" included whites. My set of friends, assembled from my brief stop in the architecture school, my time in the dorm, and my four years at the student paper, was almost all white. It seemed a time when, at least for me, race could either be vaulted over or simply ignored.

When I went to San Francisco to take my first job, at the *San Francisco Chronicle,* I spent only a couple of days looking for an apartment and settled on the first one I saw that I could afford—a modest but well-kept flat in a narrow, Victorian-style townhouse. I hardly even noticed the surrounding area. In fact, it wasn't until I was moving in that I realized I would be living smack in the middle of the Western Addition, one of the city's biggest black neighborhoods.

The truth is that I didn't know just what I felt about that. This was a big city, and I'd never lived in Urban Black America before. I knew what it was, having spent summer internships working cub reporter jobs in Washington and Detroit, but I'd never resided there. In every sense, this was a long way from Ann Arbor and an even longer way from Orangeburg.

It was an education. I learned how to get around by bus (not being able to afford a car). I learned how to exist in a local economy that didn't run on credit cards or personal checks. I learned what now seem elementary things, like how to walk down a dark street, maybe the wrong dark street, with the proper degree of swagger and attitude to minimize your chance of being hassled in any way. The trick is to stride tall, puff yourself up, be big and bad—but not so big and bad that you pose a disrespectful challenge. It helps to be six-four.

I learned how to shop at corner grocery stores that stocked stubbornly ungentrified food: fatty cuts of meat; off-brand canned goods; household items packaged so you could buy one sponge or one roll of toilet paper. Stores, in other words, where most customers' purchases were likely to be governed not by some conceptual budget, but by the concrete fact of how many dollar bills they had in their pockets at the moment of entering the store.

On the bus and on the street corners I heard people talking, for the first time, about playing the numbers. I never played, though, because I never heard anybody talk about winning. I eavesdropped with a reporter's ear whenever I went to the local laundromat, and heard myriad tales of woe—financial, romantic, legal, spiritual, medical, any kind of woe you could imagine. I paid a lot of attention to the faces I saw on the street, hard city faces, game-day faces; it took a while before I could see past them to the humanity inside.

The humanity: This was a different kind of black life from the life I'd known in Orangeburg, certainly much faster paced, much more aggressive and edgy, but at the same time more open and engaging and accessible, and in some ways more inclusive. The best word to describe it is promiscuous, but not in the sexual sense; rather, in the sense of life's being all mingled and disorderly and random. I'd set out for the store to buy some coffee, bump into somebody I knew (or didn't know) at the bus stop, have a conversation about the Forty-Niners or the weather or the impending wrath of Jehovah, detour to the African boutique, get chased out by the incense, bump into somebody else who wanted to invite me to a neighborhood meeting or a church service, suddenly remember the coffee, find that the store was out of my brand and end up talking to the manager—whatever you set out to do, you ended up doing what you ended up doing. Schedules were a compromise between clock time and the rhythm of life.

It was the only time in my life when "the projects" were not a distant abstraction but a local landmark, a place where I recognized people to wave at when I walked past and they waved back.

I was a little unsettled for a time, and then I came to love it. I felt like a spy able to move effortlessly between two worlds. I'd spend my days participating in the white world of work downtown, and then I'd get on the McAllister trolley bus and ride home and just blend in, and by the time I reached my stop I was in another world, a black world. This may sound trivial, but it was the first time I'd actually commuted between worlds, every single day, participating in both of them. It was like having a second identity, a second existence. The Gene Robinson known to the lady behind the counter at the corner store didn't have to have anything to do with the Gene Robinson known to the lady behind the counter at the kiosk in the *Chronicle*'s lobby.

Ultimately, though, I got a raise and the flat began to seem too small, and so I moved. I was living in the upper Haight-Ashbury—a white neighborhood—by the time I met Avis.

She was in San Francisco for postgraduate study, and she'd ended up living in a house with a group of people—all of them white—who all either co-owned or worked in a coffee shop near Golden Gate Park called the Sacred Grounds. (This was 1976, after all.) A friend of mine from Michigan—also white—moved to San Francisco and by chance ended up living in that same house. Yes, I met my love at the Sacred Grounds. After we got together, in search of ever-better apartments, we moved from my white neighborhood to a house in an even whiter neighborhood with a view, and then finally to the Mission District, which was mostly Latino.

When we came to Washington, our housing choices were narrowed. Avis had grown up in Silver Spring, in the Maryland suburbs, and her family still lived there, so she ruled out Maryland on the principle that it was good to be close to family, but not on top of them. She also wasn't keen on living in the District of Columbia itself because of the rising crime rate, even though my job was to be covering the mayor. That left Virginia, so we looked for places in Arlington, which seemed as close to the city as we could get.

Without much trouble we found a place in a hilly, pleasant, upscale, pretty much exclusively white neighborhood called Country Club Hills. That name was the first bad sign: "country club," in Orangeburg, had been a code word for a whole set of privileges that were forbidden to people with skin like mine; at Orangeburg High, on Monday mornings, I'd had to endure hearing white classmates talk about the golf or tennis or swimming they'd enjoyed over the weekend at the "country club," always the "country club," and I didn't even know where the damn thing was. But Country Club Hills seemed pleasant enough, and the house was adequate as a rental while we got our bearings, so we decided to take it.

I remember driving out to sign the lease. We had to take a road called Old Dominion—a second bad sign, in my view—to the realty office in the ritzy suburb of McLean. The secretary showed us in. Avis and I sat there doing the paperwork, aware of a certain unfocused tension in the air, until finally the boss stopped and looked at us across the table.

"Now you realize," he said, searching somewhat painfully for the words, "that you'll be the first . . . the first . . ."

I honestly don't recall if he ever managed to finish that sentence. Yes, we were the first black people to live on our block, and no, we never received a visit from the Welcome Wagon. It wasn't really our kind of place, to say the least.

One of our neighbors was a man we called the Lawn Nazi—we anticipated Seinfeld and soup by nearly a decade—who seemed to live for his lawn. Twice a week, at least, he could be seen marching behind his mower, manicuring each blade of grass, making vertical lines with his passes on Saturday mornings, then horizontal lines on Wednesday afternoons. I'd drive home and see him out there and I'd wave, but he never waved back. The truth is that none of the neighbors did.

We only stayed in that house a year, but in a perverse sense we enjoyed being there, if only for the sake of—well, for the sake of being there. Not so many years ago outright racial segregation in housing had been perfectly legal and perfectly commonplace in Virginia and throughout the South. Both Avis and I believed it was a good thing for these white people, especially the Lawn Nazi, to have black neighbors. We both grew up in integrationist times, and there was an element of defiance in the way we approached life. We had the right to be there, and so, damn it, we were going to be there.

For me, it was the opposite of the experience I had when I first moved to San Francisco. This time, I worked downtown in a black setting all day, among the black politicians and officials at the District Building or out in Washington's black neighborhoods, and then at night I came home to a white suburban setting. It was a good arrangement, in the sense of providing an escape from the pressure-cooker atmosphere in which I worked. But it was also a bit schizophrenic, and a bit lonely. Being unique in the neighborhood meant feeling exposed, and this sensation of nakedness was often uncomfortable. I felt under constant scrutiny in a way I wouldn't feel again until many years later, in Buenos Aires, when people would stare and point when my family and I walked down the street.

We left Country Club Hills, not unhappily, to buy our first house in a cheaper, funkier part of Arlington.

Black friends of mine at work thought I was crazy. Virginia, the seat of the old Confederacy, had been in many ways as hostile to black people as any state in the South. Long after Maryland and even Washington itself had opened their doors and stores and public accommodations to African Americans, Virginia had remained closed. Black people who'd grown up in the area had memories at least that long, and thought that any black man who voluntarily lived in Virginia—who even went so far as to buy a house there, putting down roots—needed to have his head examined.

Other black colleagues thought that since my job was to cover the District of Columbia, I had a duty to live there, taking the bad along with the good. Still others thought that if I were de-

termined to live in the suburbs then that was my right, but that
the place I had to go was Prince George's County, Maryland,
which was rapidly becoming a center of suburban black affluence. If I wasn't willing to help shore up a declining black community in the inner city, then at least I should help build a rising
black community in the suburbs.

But Avis and I liked Arlington. Our new neighborhood
hadn't yet gentrified; we lived next to working-class whites,
across the street from apartment houses populated by blacks and
Latinos, within easy walking distance of a rock 'n' roll bar called
Whitey's, a great Chinese restaurant, and a Vietnamese business
strip known as Little Saigon. Our house was close-in and afford-
able, and it promised to be a good investment. We didn't really
doubt our choice.

Shortly before we went overseas, though, we traded up.
Aaron had arrived, and suddenly our little house was far too small.
We looked and looked and didn't find anything we could swing,
and were close to giving up when Avis took a colleague's advice
and drove through an Arlington neighborhood called Tara and
found the house we'd been looking for—a big white colonial with
classic lines, real shutters, and enough room for a growing family.

The thought of living in a place called Tara was, in great measure, horrifying. My years in Orangeburg had robbed me of any
patience whatsoever for romantic allusions to the Old South.
Avis felt the same way; she flatly refused to consider any house,
any house at all, that had columns meant to evoke those antebel-
lum plantation manors.

On the other hand, though, there was a certain irony in the
name. And the neighborhood itself was lovely—hilly, full of dog-
woods and azaleas, bereft of traffic, quiet and secluded yet within
an easy walk of restaurants and stores.

It was all-white, though — not a black person in sight.

The house felt right and, at the same time, I felt we might be taking another step deeper into white suburbia, and I wondered if that was really the direction we wanted to head — if we really wanted to move back toward dreaded Country Club Hills. "Conflicted" would have been the diagnosis of any reputable housing shrink.

Avis and I laughed and joked about our new neighborhood — at the Chaplinesque double-takes our new neighbors had done when they got their first look at the newcomers, at the awkwardness of their introductions, at their apparent struggle to decide just what to make of us. At the same time, though, we felt a bit lost in this big old house we could barely afford. And we felt a bit isolated. Our old Arlington neighborhood had been the kind where people sat on their front stoops drinking beer in the evenings. In Tara, if people had had front stoops, they certainly wouldn't have sat on them, and certainly not drinking beer. Our neighbors tended to be older, tended to keep mostly to themselves — nice people, as far as we could tell, but hardly demonstrative. At our old house, our next-door neighbors — they were white, by the way — had driven us to the hospital when Avis was about to deliver Aaron. It was hard to imagine who, among the pleasant retirees of Tara, would offer a similar service.

Our isolation was not just because of factors like age and unfamiliarity, but also because of race. We stood out in a way that we'd found uncomfortable in Country Club Hills, and there was a question — unstated, but there nonetheless — of whether this degree of isolation was sustainable in the long term.

Before we could address any of these questions we moved away to South America. There we got some answers, but only partial ones.

The real point, I suppose, is that for every dwelling I've ever lived in I can easily recall the racial composition of the neighborhood, of the surrounding city, even of the surrounding metropolitan area. The race of my neighbors was an important part of the context of wherever I was living at the time, and I couldn't have failed to notice it, record it, analyze it, and adjust my attitudes and expectations accordingly. For better or worse, race always mattered.

MAC MARGOLIS WANTED me to see another side of Rio de Janeiro — a side of the city that had nothing to do with the perfect beaches and the stunning views — so he took me to a place called Rocinha, which was generally considered the biggest slum in the Americas.

It is a vast, improvised city-within-a-city slung in the broad saddle between two dramatic peaks overlooking Rio's southern beaches. I noticed, of course, that the place was dirt-poor, with its houses of cinderblock and plywood and corrugated tin. I sensed immediately, from having spent some time in American ghettos, that it was fairly dangerous. We were extremely careful where we went and whom we talked to.

In my earlier trips to the favelas, I'd been struck by the fact that they weren't exclusively black, the way inner-city ghettos tend to be in the United States. Now, though, in Rocinha I saw something else. I saw clearly how few whites there were. This may have escaped the notice of many of the two hundred thousand or so people who lived there, and certainly didn't seem to mean much to the larger society, but Rocinha was indeed almost entirely black, like that little town Planaltina had been.

In fact, from certain places on the hillside, you could look out and see the entire racial structure of the metropolis. The beaches,

all public, were racially mixed—whites pulling up for an afternoon of sun and sand in their cars, blacks arriving by bus or on
foot, some having walked down from Rocinha and the other
slums or taken the bus in their swimsuits and rubber sandals. The
apartment buildings along the beaches and in the expensive flat-
land neighborhoods were all white, except for the doormen and
the maids and the garderners. The slums, which ironically enjoyed all the most spectacular views, were where the black people
lived. Going uphill was like going to another world.

There was of course an economic component to all of this.
Rich people live in the fancy areas, poor people in the slums. But
it was no longer possible for me to chalk it all up to economics, all
the de facto segregation I saw. Just as it had in the neighborhoods I'd lived in, race mattered.

ONCE I SPENT a day as a tourist in the world of Brazilian crime.
For a story, I tagged along with a reporter and two photographers who worked for a lurid Rio newspaper called *O Povo* ("The
People") that survived on crime news and nothing else. The theory was all blood and guts, all the time. The reporter was a sweet-
faced, gentle-voiced woman named Lucia Tavares whose job,
basically, was to get up early each morning and dash around to
inspect as many of the night's fresh corpses as possible before the
police got there to haul them away. She didn't particularly seem
to like this, but didn't seem to mind it much either; it was a job,
and jobs were hard to come by. I was sickened and appalled, and
a lot of my anger had to do with race.

It was a cool, gray, damp day, the air filled with a heavy mist
on the verge of condensing into drizzle. Our driver, a black man
named Amaury, confidently threaded far away from the glittering

beaches through a back-alley maze to a freeway heading into the heart of what the *cariocas* called the North Zone, then off into a neighborhood where wooden shacks lined a fetid canal. Finally the car emerged onto an avenue lined with car repair shops and warehouses, and Amaury slowed to hunt for the right address.

There, in front of a graffiti-covered wall, we found the first corpse of the day, curled in the fetal position and all wrapped up like a work by some Christo-groupie art student with a macabre sense of humor: the first layer a baby-blue shower curtain festooned with smiling sea horses, then a clear plastic sheet, then assorted plastic grocery bags, the whole assemblage held together by lashings of black electrical wire tied in elaborate knots. From underneath seeped a trickle of blood. A single police officer stood sentry, waiting for the overworked forensic team to arrive.

"Looks like Caverinha's work," Lucia said to the cop. She explained to me that Caverinha was the professional name of a local drug trafficker whose business disputes often culminated in the discovery of bundles like this one.

"Has all the signs," the cop replied. "Wrapped like a ham."

"Funny thing, though," Lucia noted idly. "Caverinha usually uses yellow wire."

The cop shrugged, not missing a beat. "Must have run out."

An hour later, after the technicians had come and the unwrapping was complete, the victim turned out to be a young black man of around twenty, with medium-brown skin and reddish-brown hair. He was wearing a green army jacket over a black shirt and gray warm-up pants. Someone had shot him a dozen times, after slashing his face with a razor and burning his chest with cigarettes. I never found out his name, and nobody ever found out why he had been killed.

Next, on instructions from Lucia's editor, we went off wandering through a neighboring slum in search of a murdered baby. Mercifully, we couldn't find the address.

Then we were dispatched across town to Mineira, one of the toughest favelas in town. Starting downtown at the Sambadrome, the grandstand where Rio's grand, glittering *carnaval* parade is held each year, we climbed narrow streets and snaked around the hillside until finally the road petered out. Amaury refused to try to go any farther—he was responsible for the company car and feared what might happen to it—so the only way to continue was on foot. Every city editor in the world knows that while reporters and photographers are expendable, cars are not.

The favela was a jumble of narrow corridors and steep stairways, blind alleys and steep drop-offs where pungent tongues of garbage spilled down the hill. In a narrow lane, protected from view by walls of corrugated metal, we came across a dozen policemen hiding from a group of heavily armed drug traffickers who were standing on a rooftop on another hill about two hundred yards away.

At the end of this lane there were more cops, and then, finally, lying on a flat rooftop below, was the body of a young black man who had been shot at least ten times. The police said his name was Robson dos Anges; nobody in the neighborhood was willing to admit seeing or hearing anything. Nobody was even willing to admit living there.

We kept cruising and kept finding bodies, and there was a pattern—we were finding young black bodies. This was not an unfamiliar exercise, or an unfamiliar result. I'd done similar duty myself on the night police beat in San Francisco, where I'd seen my first dead body—a black man shot and dumped behind San Francisco General Hospital. Before, I'd always thought I'd be sickened by the sight of a dead body, but I wasn't; the truth is that it left me numb, completely numb. The city of Washington, during my years there, had been working hard to become the murder capital of the nation. I'd served a time as city editor, in charge of the coverage of local Washington. I'd enforced the policy that every homicide, no matter who the victim, rated at least a brief mention in the paper. We ran story after story about the crisis, and the coverage made many white suburbanites increasingly afraid to come into the city. The truth was, though, that they needn't have worried: Virtually all the victims of Washington's murder epidemic were young black men, and virtually all of them were shot to death by other young black men.

But there was a difference, a big difference. In Washington, the rising murder rate was seen specifically as a crisis in the black community—an epidemic of black-on-black murder. The search for solutions was framed in terms that explicitly took that racial element into account. Those solutions were not working—the murder rate, at the time, was still rising, and it would require broader demographic trends to bring it down—but at least race established a context for viewing and analyzing what was going on. The victims were black, the murderers were black, and black people had a lower status in the society. It was something we could grab onto, a reference point we could use to begin to explain a wave of nihilistic carnage that otherwise would have been inexplicable. It was a starting point we could use to try to make things better.

In Brazil, though, there was no such context for the violence. There was poverty, but that didn't explain very much in a nation where so much of the population—most of it, in fact—was poor, much poorer than the inhabitants of America's urban ghettos. Still, no one offered any other explanation. Neither Lucia nor her editors nor the photographers nor the cops made the slightest mention of the fact that all the corpses we saw in Rio that day were black corpses. Nobody drew any inference at all.

Nobody, that is, but me. The inference I drew was that young black men were seen as expendable in Brazil; that they were seen as likely not to have much education or many prospects; that they were seen as likely to be involved in some kind of criminal activity; that they were seen as a threat to whites; and that when they were murdered they were seen as perhaps deserving their fate, perhaps not, but in any case nothing to get too worked up about. I was ready to get on my high horse about all this, until on reflection I realized that that could be a pretty good description of the way young black men were seen in the United States as well.

The lack of acknowledgment still bothered me, though. It bothered me that nobody saw these neighborhoods that were running with blood as *black* neighborhoods. Nobody saw that blood that was flowing as *black* blood. Nobody but me.

Chapter 8

Carnaval

I'D MADE A PROMISE TO MYSELF SOON AFTER MY FIRST TRIP TO Brazil, the solemn pledge that I would not be the first South America correspondent so stupid that he never went to *carnaval* in Rio. February was nearing, so I dreamed up an excuse to satisfy my editors, wangled myself a hotel room, and then called Mac Margolis and announced that I was coming. I'd been looking forward to what everyone said was one of the greatest spectacles in the world, and I was looking forward to having Mac as my guide.

"That's great," he said, with the dripping ennui of a world-weary German intellectual in the 1920s. "I'll tell you everything you need to know. You're welcome to the office, anything you need. I won't be here, though. I'll be out of town. The truth is that I always try to leave town during *carnaval*. But you'll have a great time, really you will."

I should have taken that as a warning, I suppose, or at least a clue. My best friend in Rio, someone whose experience and judgment I'd always relied on, made a habit of leaving town during the week that all good *cariocas* looked forward to more than any other. That shouldn't have added up. But there wasn't time to stop to think about it. If Mac had his own reasons for avoiding *carnaval*, then that was his business. I was not about to skip it myself.

If I had, I would have missed the greatest spectacle I've ever seen, but that's almost incidental. More important, I would have also missed the moment when I knew—deep in the gut, deep in the soul—that the way in which Brazil looked right through race without really seeing it was wrong for me. I'd have missed the moment when the incredible sense of freedom I had when I was in Brazil, the sense of weightlessness, the sense of living without lines, the sense of new possibilities that I'd felt that first time on the beach in Rio suddenly disappeared, leaving me adrift in a void.

I'd have missed the day when the last of my illusions finally died. But I'd also have missed the day when I first began to realize how rich, how full, how valuable the *old* possibilities could be.

ON THE RIDE from the airport to Copacabana the city didn't look any different; there was nothing to indicate that this was a special time of the year. But as soon as I got settled in my hotel and started making a few phone calls, the difference became obvious. It was a Thursday afternoon, and none of the people I wanted to interview were in their offices. "Back next Wednesday," all the secretaries said. By four o'clock, even the secretaries had left and the phones just went unanswered.

I went out for a walk and ended up at a little place I knew in Ipanema where you could sit outside and have a beer. I was just settling in when a pattern of regular drumbeats began to emerge from the usual loud chaos of Rio's street noise, a samba beat that got louder and louder until suddenly—I'm still not sure from where, exactly—a parade had materialized.

It was just a spontaneous neighborhood celebration, a kind of warm-up for the revelry yet to come—*carnaval* wouldn't officially begin until the following day, Friday. But this was magical. About three hundred people were marching down the street, most of them in swimsuits but some in elaborate costume, propelled by drummers who'd organized themselves into an ad hoc *bateria,* or drum corps, pounding their big bass drums and their snares and their tiny handheld *pandeiros* in a kind of syncopated unison.

They were dancing and singing a samba, doubtless the theme song of one of the major samba schools that would march in the weekend competition. I didn't recognize the piece, but everybody else on the restaurant terrace seemed to. People at other tables joined in; the people in the parade cheered; the people in the restaurant cheered back; and soon, the parade had halted and just kind of engulfed the restaurant. People in tights and angel's wings and lots of glitter were suddenly snaking among the tables, singing and laughing and demonstrating the national genius for celebration.

"*Meu nome é Gal!*" someone yelled in my ear.

I turned and found myself nose to nose with a tall drag queen in a leopard-skin bikini. "What?" I said.

"*Meu nome é Gal! Meu nome é Gal! Meu nome é Gal!*"

It took me a moment to get my bearings—she was tall, drunk, and a little bit hairy—before I realized that she was saying her name was "Gal," which apparently meant that she was dressed and made up to look like the singer Gal Costa. I didn't see the resemblance, but there was no need to tell her that.

"Your name is Gal," I said.

"*Sim! Sim! Meu nome é Gal!*" And then the hirsute Gal Costa tottered away on her high heels, waving a feathered boa above her head.

Even in Rio, that sort of thing didn't happen every day. *Carnaval* had arrived.

What happens is that the whole city—the whole country, really—essentially stops functioning for the five days leading up to Ash Wednesday and the beginning of Lent. It's basically the same pre-Lenten blowout that's held in Venice, Trinidad, New Orleans, and other places around the world, but in Brazil it's incomparably bigger, bolder, badder. Also, in Brazil, it falls in late summer, not the dead of winter as in the northern hemisphere. On Friday in Rio comes the official kickoff with the introduction of Rei Momo, the king of *carnaval*. On Friday night and Saturday night there are big annual *carnaval* balls held in various auditoriums, affairs that compete to outdo one another in glitz, celebrity, heat, and raunch. On Sunday and Monday the big samba school competition is held in the Sambadrome downtown. On Tuesday, the winning school performs an encore parade. And on Wednesday morning everyone wakes up with a punishing hangover; a few souls even make it to church.

The generic pre-Lenten carnival is a function of the Christian calendar, and so in that sense it's European, but the Brazilian *carnaval*—the drumming, dancing, delirious celebration in the streets—has its roots in the black neighborhoods of Salvador, the blackest of Brazil's major cities. Many Brazilians and old-hand expatriates, like Mac, complain that Rio's *carnaval* has become too Las Vegas and too white, and they say that for the true experience you have to go to Salvador. That may be true, but it's also true that there's nothing bigger or more mind-blowing than *carnaval* in Rio. It's the Super Bowl, the Mt. Everest, the World War II of parties, the standard against which all others are measured and found wanting.

It's hard to explain the feeling of *carnaval* in Rio. All businesses, except those servicing revelers and tourists, are closed. Streets are blocked off. The quantities of beer and liquor consumed are unimaginable. In the age of AIDS, condom sales go through the roof. Everyday norms of behavior are suspended — you don't ask, and you certainly don't tell. If it happened during *carnaval*, it didn't really happen at all. You jam with drummers on the beach even if you've never struck a drum in anger before. You open yourself to people in a way that would be unthinkable and highly unwise at any other time of the year. Everyone is your friend; no man is an island. Barriers come down: Bankers hold hands with their maids and samba down the street, while tipsy housewives are spun and twirled by their gardeners. Mild-mannered office workers walk the streets in outrageous drag, not worried in the least about running into their bosses — who might be in drag as well. You party desperately until you run out of steam, then regroup and party some more. You sing, you shout, you dance with strangers until dawn.

It took me a couple of days, but I got into the mood. I didn't have a costume, but I did have an African-patterned shirt and pants that I'd thrown into the suitcase, and so I put that outfit on like a new persona and went out to a couple of the *carnaval* balls.

The first, at a place called Scala, was an upper-crusty affair at an auditorium in the fanciest, most expensive part of town. It was a celebrity ball, a place where starlets and soccer stars and other members of the glitterati came to see and be seen. People wore outrageous costumes: There were catwomen, Roman centurions, and androgynous beings so weighted down with their towering headdresses and their golden robes that they could barely move. Bare breasts were common, and they were perfect bare breasts, shaped by Rio's best plastic surgeons. The samba band was professional, one of the best in town; the decoration was slick and flashy. I stayed until one or two in the morning, and the party was just heating up, but there was something missing; everyone seemed to be playing to the cameras—the Brazilian television networks covered the major balls like the Oscars—and the chemistry just didn't ignite for me.

The next night I went to another ball at a place called Monte Libano, a ball that, despite also taking place in the upscale part of town, has a reputation as a much more working-class celebration. This was more like it.

Admission was just a few bucks, a quarter of what I'd paid at Scala. The crowd pushing to get through the doors was livelier, more active, less concerned about appearances; not as many people were in costume, and hardly anyone looked to have dressed for the cameras. Not that there were any cameras.

I went inside and immediately found myself in the middle of the dance floor, and the only way to cross it—the bar, and the beer, were on the other side—was to dance my way across. Bodies were packed indecently tight; those that were bare, or mostly bare, were as God had made them and not as the surgeons might have remade them. The band played nonstop, running through all the year's samba theme songs without so much as a pause between numbers. Couples were dancing, triples, individuals, groups. Everyone seemed drunk or otherwise stoned. It was hot and humid, sticky and oppressive, and the air was sweet-and-sour with sweat and cologne.

This was a house party run amok. In one dark corner, a man was passed out; in another, a man and a woman seemed to be making love. There was a fistfight outside, but the two guys were both too drunk to do much damage. A couple had a terrible row that ended when the man shoved the woman to the floor and the woman threw something at him and stormed away; later, when I went outside to the terrace to get some air, I saw them walking arm-in-arm.

It was a blast and I stayed until four. It wasn't until much later in the day, after breakfast and a lot of Tylenol, this distinction registered: The party at Scala had been mostly white, while the one at Monte Libano had been mostly black.

ON SUNDAY NIGHT came the main event: I went to the Sambadrome.

The way it works is that all year the top sixteen samba schools prepare their *carnaval* presentations, and over two nights they compete to win the championship—and a year's bragging rights for the school's neighborhood and its supporters. They are judged on the quality of the samba song they've commissioned, the depth of the theme they've chosen to explore, the craftsmanship and inventiveness of the floats, the caliber of the celebrities they've recruited to ride along, the beauty and outrageousness of the costumes, the musicianship of the drumming, the skill of the dancing, the overall choreography, the overall enthusiasm, the overall spectacle.

Until a few years ago, the parade competition was held on a major avenue in the city center. But *carnaval* had gotten bigger and gone upscale, and now the venue for the contest is the Sambadrome, several blocks of a downtown street that are lined with a giant permanent grandstand designed by Oscar Niemeyer, the same architect who designed all the most important buildings of Brasília. I have a hard time thinking of another nation that would commission one of the major figures of twentieth-century architecture to design a facility for judging how well competing organizations party-hearty.

The schools slowly parade through, with their towering allegorical floats and their brilliantly costumed multitudes, the marchers singing and dancing until they pass the end of the grandstand and spill out into a giant plaza called the Apotheosis. Up to five thousand people parade for each school; it takes an hour and a half, more or less, for each school to run the gauntlet.

A cab dropped me as close to the Sambadrome as possible, which was about five blocks away. The neighborhood was dicey, and I wouldn't have relished walking there alone any other time of the year, but tonight it was so thronged that the only danger was from pickpockets and I didn't have anything in my pockets but enough cash to get through the evening anyway. It was the most surreal twilight stroll I've ever taken. Spectators and participants were all streaming in the same direction, so that for a while I'd walk amid a normal-looking crowd, and then suddenly I'd be among a group of cave people wearing glitter-encrusted loincloths, or a bunch of bright red devils with horns and tails. Eventually, the two crowds diverged; those marching in the parades went to the staging areas, and the rest of us made our way to the grandstand.

I was alone, but in Rio during *carnaval* you're never really alone. My reserved seat, practically in the front row, was in a box along with an obviously wealthy young white couple and a two middle-aged mulatto women. Within seconds, as is customary at *carnaval* time, we were all best friends, even though my Portuguese was still fairly shaky and there was so much noise that I couldn't hear what anyone was saying anyway.

It was an incredible night. The assault of color and rhythm begins around seven in the evening and lasts until seven the next morning. Themes vary: one school might be doing a historical pageant on slavery, while another might be riffing on the wonders of drunkenness. Costumes vary according to the theme in question and the school's official colors—and, of course, the imagination of the *carnaval* impresario in charge.

But some elements of the form are standard. Each school's parade begins with a group of older men from the neighborhood dressed in sparkling finery, suspenders and bow ties and the like, often making them look, frankly, almost minstrelish. Each school has A-list celebrities lending cachet to the parade, the select and the famous often perched stories high atop elaborate floats—volcanoes, Gardens of Eden, city skylines, all trundling down the route at a stately pace. Each school has as its starring performers a special couple, a woman who carries the school flag and her consort, and they do a whirling dance distinct from the samba that most everyone else is doing. Each school has hordes of organizers and helpers who hover around the parade like worker bees, keeping the lines straight and the formations tight and exhorting the nonchalant to greater enthusiasm, perhaps even winning enthusiasm.

And each school has a group, or "wing," of Bahianas— women from the neighborhood, older women, grandmothers. Their costumes consist of voluminous white dresses of Salvador lace, traditional Bahian costume, over vast crinoline petticoats. There are hundreds of them, coming down through the Sambadrome in a bloc, and they whirl in unison as they march, making the dresses billow like the skirts of dervishes. Their appearance is one of the signature moments of each school's parade, a constant, a returning to roots. It is a beautiful contrast, white lace and dark skin—most of these women are dark.

Because Avis and I had made that trip to the Salgueiro samba school's headquarters, I'd chosen the night when I knew Salgueiro would be among the groups marching. When the first school came dancing through, I didn't quite know how to react. With the second, I got into the whole thing a little more; and by the time the third came past, its theme song a witty little ditty about drunkenness, I was singing along like the rest of the vast crowd, having memorized the words: *"Hoje vou tómar um porre, não me socorre, que `tou feliz . . ."*

By the time Salgueiro entered the Sambadrome, a vast sea of red and white, I knew how to pay attention to what was going on. I knew how to look through the spectacle and see inside. Maybe I'd learned too well. Because when Salgueiro's wing of Bahianas came by, the whole experience of *carnaval*—and of Brazil—changed for me. I was no longer seeing an extravaganza, I was seeing people. I was seeing a society.

Sitting almost in the front row, I was spellbound as the Bahianas from Salgueiro came past. But then, suddenly and without intending to, I stopped looking at the costumes and the artistic contrast, and began looking at the people as individuals. I was within just a few feet of some of these women: I looked at their faces. I saw the lines that creased their brows; I saw the uneven, gapped teeth; I saw the cloudiness of their eyes. They whirled as if they would float away, but I saw the heaviness of their legs and the toughness of their feet, burdened feet.

I saw their bodies, imperfect bodies that told their own histories, some too thin, many too fat, all with the sags and bulges that come from a combination of frequent childbearing and constant hard labor. Looking past the joy and glory of the moment, I saw hard lives.

These women looked frightfully old, but poverty adds phantom years; a few might have been as young as their fifties, but most seemed certainly to be in their sixties and a few in their seventies. On this hot, humid evening they were dancing to a fast samba, prodded by the worker bees to dance harder and faster, whirling their dresses and smiling their crooked smiles and singing the Salgueiro samba as if their lives depended on it.

"One of these women is going to drop dead of a heart attack," I blurted out in English.

"Don't worry about them," said the male half of the young white couple to my right—I hadn't realized he spoke English. "They're used to working hard. They're tough old ladies."

The instant those words were out of his mouth, my whole view of the spectacle changed.

I didn't say anything aloud. To myself, I said: Those are *black* women.

Black women.

Of course, that was self-evident. And yet—and yet in a sense it wasn't self-evident, at least not until that very moment. I realized that I couldn't see them clearly, couldn't see their situation clearly, their lives, their dreams, their pasts and futures, without that adjective: black. I couldn't know them just as old women, or poor women, or Salgueiro women. They were black, and black was more than just a color. It was a condition. It was an identity about which some of them might have been ambivalent, that some of them might even have rejected, but that suddenly, for me, had a clarity and a pertinence that changed everything.

Those women marching in the heat in those beautiful frilly white dresses, like so many others in the parades for all the samba schools, were black. The parades certainly were not exclusively so, but largely so: You could pick out those who really lived in the neighborhoods, and they tended to be black, while those who were supporters but lived in tonier precincts (they were the ones having trouble with the steps) tended to be white.

The people way back at other end of the Sambadrome, looking down on the festivities from a highway overpass because they couldn't afford a ticket—they tended to be black, too. The people in the steep, open grandstand were a mix, but if you unfocused your eyes and took in a general impression of color you could see they were mostly light-skinned or white. The people in the box seats, where I was sitting, were mostly white.

My ticket had cost a hundred fifty dollars, at the time about three times the minimum monthly wage.

From then on, when I thought about race in Brazil and tried to make sense of it in relation to race in America, I thought of those Bahianas from Salgueiro. What I'd seen was a group of proud, beautiful black women, marching in an expression of black Brazilian culture. I'd seen a clear pattern of racial stratification. I'd seen economic and political disparities; I'd heard the empowered dismiss the unempowered with unthinking disdain. I'd seen a situation that, in a lawyer's terminology, was actionable.

And yet most of the people there with me that night hadn't seen those things at all. They'd seen blacks and whites and browns coming together in the world's biggest, most spectacular, most entertaining street party. They'd seen the color and the pageantry, the nudity, the celebrity, the glitz. They had enjoyed themselves; I had, too. I wouldn't have missed that evening for the world.

But that was the beginning of the end of my infatuation for the idea that if you refuse to acknowledge race, somehow you can make it just go away. The process of realization had been going on for some time anyway, but that night was when I began to put it together, when I came to understand that structuring a society so that black people didn't "have to be" black didn't seem to do much good for black people at all. That, in fact, it seemed to do them harm, to hold them down—worse, to deny them even the awareness that they were being held down, to deny them the language to talk about it and the anger to do something about it. Amid all the beauty and excitement and joy of that evening, I saw something that was backward and ugly and wrong.

And I still see those women whirling like dervishes, white lace billowing around sturdy black legs, a study in contrast.

I STAYED ALL NIGHT at the Sambadrome. Around two or three in the morning, as the fifth or sixth samba school was marching past, I stopped participating, except for the occasional cheer, and instead just let the sights and sounds wash over me. The others in my box were still going strong, dancing and cheering and guzzling beer, but I just sat there, entranced, overwhelmed, perturbed, forever changed.

It was dawn when I walked out through the Apotheosis and back into the normal world, amid a spent tide of fairy princesses, angels with broken wings, puffy-eyed Cleopatras, sagging Adonises, and barefooted bare-breasted nymphets clutching themselves against the morning's slight chill.

I spent my last *carnaval* evening downtown at what some of my Rio friends assured me was the most authentic event of the whole week, the Avenida Rio Branco parade.

This was a showcase for the second-tier and third-tier samba schools, the ones not quite ready for prime time. The big difference was that it was still held in the streets, like the big Sambadrome competition used to be. I'd been told that here I would see the true spirit of *carnaval*—the grassroots joy, the improvised creativity, the power and the warmth and the indomitability.

But that's not at all that I saw. Maybe I was just partied out by this point. Maybe I'd been spoiled by the slick professionalism of my night at the Sambadrome. Maybe I just couldn't shake that image of the Bahianas whirling so desperately.

I must have arrived around eight or nine at night. Central Rio, so far from the perfect beaches and the glittering high-rises, always has a sinister, dangerous feeling after dark, and even *carnaval* hadn't managed to dispel this blanketing gloom. I'd arrived by subway and had to walk a few blocks through a fading shopping area to get to the avenue. The stores, as usual at night, were shuttered with metal grates; the streets, as usual, were filthy with litter. A group of a half-dozen street children huddled in a doorway, thin, barefoot, glassy-eyed. I noticed that all of them were black.

There were temporary grandstands along part of the route, but for anyone willing to stand, the parade was free. The crowd was much less affluent than the crowd at the Sambadrome and seemed more volatile. Still, it was full of the *carnaval* spirit, even if my own was flagging.

The parade itself was almost unbearably poignant. The samba schools were smaller and poorer than the first-rank ones I'd seen the other night, with no huge financial backing from gangsters or business magnates—and no hordes of white wannabes who paid hundreds of dollars for the privilege of marching with their favorite school, thus subsidizing elaborate costumes for everybody else. These marchers came down Rio Branco in fishnet hose with runs, in drooping wings, in headdresses that listed to one side. The floats were little things that wobbled as they came past, and you could see the trucks and tractors underneath. The whole parade came to a halt for about twenty minutes when one of the floats broke down and had to be pushed out of the way.

The marchers were in ragged lines, and their choreography was lacking. But they had the spirit, all right. They danced and twirled and sang and drummed with all they had. They'd spent the better part of a year preparing for this moment and they were determined to seize it, to squeeze it, to extract from it every ounce of joy and abandon they possibly could. They were on stage, for once. For once, everything was about *them*, the whole country was about *them*.

And they were black.

As one school was passing — I can't recall its name, but it was from some poor neighborhood out near Rio's international air-port — the flag-carrier and her consort waltzed right over to where I was standing and performed their special dance. The woman was young and tall and dark, very pretty, but not bikini model gorgeous like the flag-carriers in the Sambadrome. I tried to imagine what her life was like. Had she gone to school? Did she have a job? Did she have children? How did she keep them fed and clothed? Was her man good to her, or had his life made him resentful, made him abusive? Tonight, for one night, this woman was the undisputed queen of her neighborhood; right now, at this moment, she was the undisputed queen of Avenida Rio Branco, whirling and bowing and whirling again on center stage. Was that pure exhilaration I saw in her eyes? Or was there also panic, at the certain knowledge that tomorrow everything — absolutely everything — would go back to the way it was?

I looked at her and I looked around and I asked myself: Why?

On one level, of course, I understood perfectly well why these poor people would spend so much time and energy and money—all of which they could hardly spare—on a few days or a few hours of unrestrained happiness. It was the same reason why poor people around the world did the same thing, why Asia's inner cities were so full of gambling dens and India's so full of brothels and Africa's so full of dance halls and America's so full of liquor stores and crack houses. If your life is bleak enough, you look for every chance to step outside of it, if only for a brief while.

But still, for me there was a sadness about that evening on Avenida Rio Branco. Maybe it was the added element of performance, the way these people put themselves on display. I felt almost like a voyeur, and not because of the many nearly naked women jiggling and prancing about. It was as if I had on a pair of those x-ray glasses that used to be advertised in comic books when I was a kid, the kind that were supposed to let you see through people's clothes. I felt as if I could see through the sequins and satin of these people's happiness to something ruined, something without hope.

Carnaval had ended.

The last samba school had danced past, and it was time to go home. I needed a cab but the streets were all blocked off, so I started walking in search of the first major thoroughfare where taxis might be trolling. The first route I chose looked iffy—too dark, not enough activity—so I reversed course and ended up at the very end of the parade route. Marchers from the various samba schools were milling about, some looking for waylaid companions, others waiting for transportation back to the favelas. A group of about a dozen men were struggling to right a float that had toppled; another group was leading another float away on foot, like a giant glittering rickshaw. No one was shouting or even talking much; it was quiet, maybe the quietest Brazilian street scene I had ever witnessed at any time of the day or night. The moment when *carnaval* ends is the fullest, most pregnant moment of the Brazilian year. The whole country is poised: After days of soaring flight, it is time to come crashing back to earth.

I made my way to an area called Cinelândia, a downtown district full of movie theaters that had fallen to seediness. The place was alive with gangs of street kids—it was where many of them lived. One group in particular caught my eye. They were sitting beneath the marquee of an old movie house showing some XXX-rated porno film, and they'd arranged themselves into a composition of pose and gesture that reminded me of the burghers of Amsterdam as depicted by Rembrandt. Some of them were achingly young, as young as my Aaron. Other spectators were wandering away from the parade in the same direction I was heading, but there was no longer any conspiracy of joy among us; we had nothing to say to one another; *carnaval* was done.

I trudged away. I felt bereft, and utterly alone.

Chapter 9

From Cream to Coal

I DIDN'T GO BACK TO BRAZIL FOR A WHILE AFTER THAT. *CARNAVAL* is a great big dose of a great big country, enough to sate even a glutton like myself. And I no longer had quite the appetite I'd once had. I no longer had a neat, optimistic framework into which I could put the place. Now, whenever I thought about Brazil, I thought immediately about the country's unacknowledged problem of race. And then, immediately after that, I thought about color. And then I didn't know *what* to think next.

So I spent some time in Buenos Aires with my family, for a change. Avis, who's never content being idle for very long, had gotten a job teaching economics and world cultures to high school students at the American school. That drew us further into an expatriate community that was doing its best to re-create a kind of Middle America on the pampas. They were mostly embassy families and corporation families; the other American journalists in town tended to be childless and thus had little participation in the lifestyle that centered on the school.

Elementary students spent half the school day learning in Spanish and the other half in English, and that's basically what the whole American expatriate culture was like, a pleasant mixture of the American and the Argentine. We'd celebrate our Fourth of July, but also the Argentine Ninth of July; we'd have barbecues of hamburgers and hot dogs, but also *asados* of Argentine beef so tender you could cut it with a butter knife; we'd drink beer, but also Mendoza red wine. A contingent of fathers took our sons' scout troop on a camping trip. We sped in a caravan out to a borrowed *estancia,* or ranch, where we pitched tents in a field and took the kids for a hike while gauchos cooked our dinner. That night, the clear sky was a carpet of stars, the Milky Way a bright wash bisecting the heavens. I'd brought along a star guide, so I pointed out the Southern Cross. In the morning, the gauchos put on a trick riding show and then let the boys take turns in the saddle.

Aaron started playing soccer, like any school-age boy in Argentina, but also got involved in the school's elaborate little league baseball program. One day, I'd take him to his soccer camp, where he tried to keep up with Argentine kids who'd dreamed since birth of becoming the next Maradona; their fathers would stand on the sidelines and scream bloody murder over a missed pass or an errant shot. The next day, I'd go to watch Aaron's little league game, and I'd watch as the pride of America's diplomatic service turned purple and apoplectic at an umpire who had had the temerity to call their kid out on strikes.

We went to church, we had dinner parties, we took excursions. And we especially got to know the other black or interracial American couples, not that there were many of them — Iris and Lou, Terry and Marie, people who eventually became long-time friends. We shared with them something we didn't share with the other Americans in Buenos Aires, the experience of being stared at on the street, the experience of being completely isolated. It forged a special bond.

And, most important of all, our family grew: We adopted Lowell.

Avis and I wanted to have another child and it just wasn't happening on its own, so we had to decide what we thought about a number of the possible options, all fraught with emotionalism, fraught with meaning, fraught with consequences both large and small—fraught with fraught, as an old editor of mine used to say. One possibility was high-tech medical intervention, but after one visit to a clinic we discovered that neither one of us was interested in pursuing that route. It was expensive, uncertain, uncomfortable, and seemed to us almost selfish in a world where there were so many children like the ones I'd see that night in Cinelândia after *carnaval,* children who needed a home.

So the choice was adoption. But that forced us to make other choices as well.

I went to Lima often, and my hotel was in a neighborhood near the U.S. consulate. Whenever I went out shopping or exploring on foot, I'd always see these American couples out strolling Peruvian babies. I knew they were American because they were big and corn-fed, they were white, they were festooned with Nike swishes, and I overheard them speaking English. The babies were dark-haired and dark-skinned, with Indian features. It took a while to dawn on me that these were adoptive parents who had come to Peru for babies, and who were passing the time in some sort of Peruvian or American legal purgatory, awaiting clearance to take their new children home.

It was a similar story in other South American countries as well—Paraguay, Colombia, even Argentina and Brazil to a lesser extent. Childless Americans, who had the means and the desire to be parents, were adopting South American babies, who were desperately in need.

But this humanitarian trend was provoking resentment and something of a backlash. There were instances in which unscrupulous lawyers had swindled either the adoptive parents or the birth mothers or both, acting essentially as baby merchants. In Peru and elsewhere, a few mothers had even come forward after the fact to claim that their babies had been stolen. Local newspapers trumpeted these cases the way they used to trumpet American political meddling, military fiddling, or other Yankee-go-home outrages. The papers were reflecting a general sullen ambivalence in most of these societies toward the whole phenomenon, toward its silent accusation that Argentina and Brazil and Peru couldn't adequately take care of their own children, their own future.

Avis and I talked about all of this. We were in South America, we knew our way around all these countries, and we knew how very great the need was. We could easily have arranged an adoption down there. But there was something about the idea that didn't seem right for us. I suppose we'd finally come to identify with our hosts. We had seen the embarrassment, the humiliation that people seemed to feel at the idea of their nations' children being taken away, even by people who had nothing but the best intentions.

We had good friends in the States who had been able to deal comfortably with these questions, adopt South American children and live happily ever after, and for them obviously it had been the right choice. But there was another factor that tipped the scale for us, and that was the fact that the need for adoptive parents—especially African-American adoptive parents—was so great at home. With most black American babies being born out of wedlock, with the African-American family in flat-out crisis, and with the inner cities in such despair, how could we *not* adopt a black child in the States?

Plus, there was family precedent. Avis's parents, despite having two boys and two girls of their own, had taken in two other boys whose parents weren't able to care for them. My grandmother, in her day, had taken in young people who'd come to Orangeburg to go to college and absorbed them into the family. I still sometimes get confused about who's really an aunt or an uncle or a cousin and who's not.

It turned out that there wasn't much of a waiting list for a black middle-class couples ready to adopt: Within six months of our having this conversation, we were flying back to Buenos Aires with a handsome three-month-old boy in our arms, Lowell Edward Robinson, the first name in honor of my father's late older brother, who'd sacrificed his own prospects to help raise his younger siblings, making it possible for them to go on to much greater things than he; and the middle name after Avis's father, whose generosity and good nature we could only wish on our new son.

Having a baby meant it was problematic for all of us to go off adventuring at the same time, but we managed to get away by twos. Avis took Aaron to the Galápagos Islands, where she took a hilarious sequence of pictures of him being chased by a sea lion jealous of his harem. I took Aaron south, to Patagonia, to see penguins and whales and towering glaciers. All of us doted on Lowell. Domesticity is hard for any foreign correspondent to manage, but for a while we came pretty close.

But there was a sense in which this felt like nothing more than an especially pleasant limbo. We were far enough into our tour to have begun thinking about whether to go home to Washington or move on to another foreign posting. I felt strongly—and Avis agreed—that it wasn't time to go home yet. I just wasn't ready to deal with all the anxiety that entailed, especially all of the anxiety that involved race.

We could debate the various options of where we might like to live, but one question I couldn't ask was where I felt I really belonged, because there wasn't a clear answer. I was an American, but I felt somehow divorced from American society. A few months earlier I'd have said that psychically and spiritually I belonged to Brazil, but that had ended in divorce as well. I was living in Argentina, and in hotel rooms and airports across South America; I belonged all those places, and at the same time I belonged nowhere.

Nowhere except with my growing family.

FAMILY: IT COMES down to sex and attraction, to white lovers and black lovers, to the contrast of brown skin and pink on crisp white sheets.

When I was growing up in Orangeburg I'm not sure I was aware that interracial relationships even existed. White people married white people, Negroes married Negroes, and that was that. At some point I must have become aware that there were a few celebrities, jazz musicians and the like, who defied convention, but they had nothing to do with my reality.

By the time I got to high school I was a little more worldly, and the world was beginning to change. Black people and white people could be friendly on television, albeit within certain parameters—Bill Cosby could carry Robert Culp's tennis gear on *I Spy*—and the developing 1960s counterculture seemed to want to be heedless of race. If black people and white people were rubbing together so closely, then black people and white people were having relationships. But not in Orangeburg—not, certainly, at Orangeburg High.

Like the other black students, I never would have thought of asking a white girl out—that went without saying. I could talk to them, of course, but not in any context that was even remotely sexual. I'm thinking especially of the "popular" girls, the cheerleaders, the blondes who were always tossing their heads to flick the golden hair from in front of their eyes. They were distant and unattainable, not even quite desirable since desire was so far out of the question. I stayed far, far away.

Once, though, I bent that rule. My "crowd" at Orangeburg High was the set of smart kids—we tended to take the same classes and participate in the same extracurricular activities. The cheerleaders were not a part of this group, which was mostly male. Some of the smart girls, those who cared most about being popular, even pretended not to be smart at all, presumably in hopes to making themselves more attractive to football captains, bankers' sons, and other prize catches. A few of the girls made no attempt to hide their brains, though, and one of the smartest was named Kathy Kovacevich. Her name itself was enough to make her an outsider at this cliqueish small-town southern school—an immigrant-sounding name, an East European name. She was good at math, she wasn't blonde, she didn't have a thick southern accent, and she had an unsaccharine quality that I found to be a refreshing change.

One afternoon we were both on our way to some meeting off-campus and I offered her a ride. She'd left something at her house and needed to pick it up, so we stopped by her house and she invited me in. I sat at her kitchen table while she fetched whatever it was, and then we left.

Nothing happened. Nothing at all. We were just acquaintances. But I remember that day intensely, because I felt like I was flirting with the ultimate danger. To be alone in a house, however briefly, with a white girl. What if her father came home? What if she accused me of something? I wasn't even attracted to her and yet the moment was sexually charged—frightening but also exhilarating, as only the truly forbidden can be.

When I went off to college in Ann Arbor, I was escaping Orangeburg and also escaping the strictures of my former life. I was young—sixteen—and just coming of age. The wider world, meaning the white world, was open to me for the first time, and I dove in. My girlfriends, when I was at Michigan, were all white.

My family was upset. When I finally settled down with a steady girlfriend and my mother asked if she was black or white, I lied: I said she was black. I'm sure my mother saw through the lie anyway, but this fiction allowed us not to talk about what to her was an obvious issue between us: that I was guilty of abandonment, gross abandonment, by not falling in love with a black woman. To me, though, there was something hard and knowing and uncompromising about black women. They seemed to see right through me. I wasn't hip, I wasn't urban-cool, I was just a kid from the South, shy around all women, vulnerable and gentle and sometimes lovesick to the point of physical pain.

By the time I moved to San Francisco, I was old enough for the thrill of being able to do whatever I wanted, with whomever I wanted, to have worn off. The selection of women with whom I had brief relationships became more varied, and for the first time since Orangeburg included black women. And then I met Avis.

We were compatible and we were in love—those are the important factors in any courtship and marriage, including ours. But as I look back on how our relationship developed, it was also important that she was a black woman who'd also become comfortable in the wider, whiter world. She'd gone to an exclusive private Catholic high school outside of Washington and then on to the University of Maryland; she'd absorbed the same cultural references that I'd absorbed in college; her circle of friends in San Francisco was more white than black.

And yet it was important to me that she was a black woman. In this, I surprised myself—since college I'd basically believed that race didn't really matter, that it was only skin deep, that it was yesterday's paradigm for looking at the world.

And yet it mattered.

It mattered that we both had grandmothers who made flaky biscuits and thick brown gravy and melt-in-your-mouth cornbread. It mattered that we both had mothers who'd joined black sororities and fathers who'd endured the separate-but-unequal rigors of military life during World War II. It mattered that we both remembered the March on Washington as a great and pivotal event, even though we were both just nine years old. It mattered that our understandings of personal history and public history coincided, that there was much we shared, that there was much we didn't have to explain to one another.

It didn't matter that we were almost exactly the same skin tone, to the point where people sometimes asked if we were brother and sister; it mattered much less that we were both physically light-medium brown than that we were both culturally and historically black, that we were both born colored, grew up as Negroes and met as a black man and a black woman, and that now we can enter middle-age together as African Americans.

It mattered, and still matters, that we have a common identity—one that happens to be based in large measure on racial identity. We didn't see color at all when we looked at one another. We saw race.

THIS WASN'T AT ALL the way I was used to thinking about our relationship. I thought we were just two people who had fallen in love and whose "race"—race being a more or less artificial construct anyhow, with no real basis in science—had nothing to do with it.

I thought Americans who talked endlessly about race, like my coworkers at the *Post,* were stuck in a loop that was taking them nowhere. I thought America's obsession with race had completely run its course and should be put to rest once and for all. I thought all our talking and arguing and fighting about race was an enormous waste of time. Race both bored me and annoyed me as a subject of discussion.

I thought Brazil had shown me a new way, thought that despite their unfortunate emphasis on color, the Brazilians were onto something. I thought that after so many years of talking about race, not talking about it was a welcome and promising change. I thought the Brazilians had found the way forward, the way out of the loop, the way for people to live together. I didn't just think it, I felt it every time I set foot in the country. I lived it, I breathed it, I knew it.

Now, though, as I puttered around Buenos Aires with my family—my black family—I came to think differently. We were a black man and a black woman; we had two black sons; we were the products of two loving extended black families.

That adjective meant something. I wasn't sure of all the things it meant, but I knew it meant something to my life, something I wanted to hold onto. It was more than just a color, or just a range of color; it went beyond that. The meaning might have been imposed by the world we lived in, for all the wrong reasons, or it might have come from within, from the purest center of my own identity. But the provenance didn't matter. Black meant more than "after midnight" or "navy blue"; black meant cream and coal and all in between; black meant me.

I WAS AT HOME in Buenos Aires when the Rodney King jury returned its verdict and Los Angeles burned. It was one of those times when we all just glued ourselves to CNN for hours on end, the whole family watching the fires burn, fascinated yet oddly detached at such a great distance, with no feel in our fingertips for whether this was the end of something or only the beginning.

A couple of days later I agreed to sit still for what I feared would be an hour of extremely public humiliation.

My friend Mariano Grondona hosted a popular television talk show, and he had asked me to be a guest several times over the years. I'd always declined, blaming my inadequate Spanish, but promised I'd do it someday. Now, salivating over the prospect of having an actual black American on his show to talk about the L.A. riots, he asked me again. In a moment of weakness I said yes.

I regretted it immediately. My Spanish was adequate for conducting interviews, but parry-and-thrust in front of the television cameras was another thing entirely. Grondona's show pulled some of the best ratings in the country, and I was sure I was about to make a fool of myself in front of several million Argentines. Live and, of course, in color.

I showed up at the studio at the appointed hour and sat down to wait alongside, I recall, a local columnist and a politician. Since I'd been in Argentina for nearly four years I shouldn't have been at all surprised by the freewheeling, improvisational nature of the furious activity around me, but I was. The show would be broadcast live, and during a commercial break I was urgently hustled across the studio floor to take my place with Grondona and the others at his round table.

I wished that earlier I'd had a Scotch instead of an espresso at the café down the street. I prayed that everybody would talk slowly enough for me to understand; my biggest fear was that someone would shoot a stream of ultra-rococo Argentine Spanish at me, heavily accented and full of slang, and I'd just sit there looking as blank as a test pattern.

Grondona, bless him, started me off with a general question that allowed me to recap the verdict and the riots, using the phrases and constructions I'd practiced—easy enough, for a start. But then he and the others began asking questions, and I realized that this was going to be even harder than I'd thought.

Not the language part; that was going pretty well. It was the context part that was giving me trouble. How do you explain a race riot to people who don't at all share your vision of race, who don't understand that vision, who don't even know there's a difference? I heard myself answering in absurd generalities.

The verdict in the Rodney King case showed that there was still racial discrimination in the United States, wasn't that right? Yes, there was still discrimination.

But things were better than they were years ago, weren't they? Yes, of course they were, for me and I supposed for most black people in the United States. But for some people they were much worse. Things were just different.

Then after all these efforts over all these years, things hadn't really changed at all? Well, no, that wasn't true. Things had changed a great deal. The fact that I was in Argentina as a foreign correspondent was clear evidence of change.

But the people obviously had a lot of anger that went beyond the case of Rodney King, didn't they? Well, yes, they obviously did.

There must be a lot of anger at Ronald Reagan and now George Bush for all their budget cuts, mustn't there? Of course there was, but that wasn't necessarily the point. It was part of the point, I supposed.

On it went in this vein, around and around and around without really getting anywhere, until finally time expired for that segment of the show and Grondona shifted the talk to some topic much closer to home. I felt relieved that it was over, but also frustrated and defeated.

I never got close to telling my questioners, and the many viewers of Grondona's popular show, what the whole Rodney King thing had looked like to me, a brown-skinned American man six thousand miles from home. I never got to tell them about sitting alone and lonely in a hotel room in Peru and seeing for the first time the videotape of King being pummeled to a pulp, watching the cops swinging from the heels like sluggers in a home-run derby, and feeling physically ill. I never got to tell how it never crossed my mind that even a white jury in white-on-white Simi Valley could find the policemen not guilty, that I never dreamed of such a thing, not one single time, until the moment the verdict was announced.

I never got to tell them how shocked I felt, how betrayed, how vulnerable, how I saw it not as some abstract threat to the American justice system or to race relations but a real bodily threat to me, personally, and in a few years my own sons. How I felt that the police officers of my country had just been given permission to pull me over for a traffic violation, drag me out of my car, and beat me half to death.

I couldn't tell them that for the first time in many years I'd felt hot, throbbing rage. I couldn't tell them how, when the riots began, part of me was egging the brick-throwers and arsonists on. I couldn't tell them that the rational part of me, the part that knew how supremely self-destructive a riot always proves to be, was muffled and obscured by a fog of anger.

I couldn't tell them that I felt, deep inside, that something needed to burn.

And above all, I couldn't tell them how I believed these seemingly poisonous feelings, at some level, were both healthy and useful. Deep, corrosive, volatile, racial anger is like rocket fuel — it can spark at the wrong moment and cause you to spectacularly self-destruct on the launching pad, or it can blast you toward a target like nothing else on earth. I've always achieved most when I was angriest.

Way back at Orangeburg High, I liked some of my teachers but hated others, precisely because they so obviously hated me and the very idea of having black students sully their pristine classrooms. Those were the classes where I excelled, where I refused to give these teachers the pleasure of marking anything wrong on my work: the geometry teacher, who tried to humiliate the black students by selectively holding them to her ostensibly classroomwide policy that she always be addressed "Ma'am"; the French teacher, who didn't seem to think blacks had the equipment to master a language of such perfection. My intention was not so much to demonstrate — to show them how wrong they were — as to embarrass them and compel them to give me my due.

I began my professional career at a time when people would say and do amazing things that stoked my inner fires for months at a time. At the *San Francisco Chronicle* I remember people expressing actual shock and amazement that I could actually write a coherent and even graceful sentence—that a young black man could put words together in a reasonable fashion. My first city editor, a little martinet who wore suspenders and a monocle, told me only after I'd moved myself and my paltry belongings all the way across the country to work for him that I wouldn't be starting off like any other reporter, that instead I'd be in a "minority training program" with a superlong probationary period. A few weeks later, he told me with some amazement, "You're one of the best black newspaper writers I've seen." He meant it as a compliment, and I'm sure he never understood why I failed to take it as such.

I understood how to make it work, though. I understood that as a black professional you withheld something from the institution that employed you. You kept a piece of yourself in reserve. With all the rest of you, you worked harder than hard and you safeguarded the company's interests at all times and you proved yourself more loyal than the average St. Bernard, all as a way of dispelling the cloud of suspicion that gathered around you because of your dark skin. But with that little bit you kept hidden away, call it the Reserve, you said to your employer, essentially, kiss my brown behind. You didn't let the Reserve buy into the company or its mission. It remained pessimistic, cynical, world-weary, and knowing. So when a disappointment came—the assignment or promotion you wanted went instead to a fair-haired boy or girl who was clearly less deserving—you could fall back on that little part of you that was mad as hell and tough as nails, and with its help you were able to shrug it off. The Reserve would put its hands on its hips and say, "Colored boy, what the *hell* did you expect?" It made you feel better, and it made you determined not just to be as good as anybody else, but twice as good.

Having that anger inside was oddly soothing. It was a weight to carry around, a heavy weight. But I could see that black Brazilians seemed to pay an awfully high price for the privilege of living without that weight. Without it, they had no sense of themselves as joined, embattled, mutually reinforced. Without it, they had no game face to show the world. Without it, they had no basis for demands, no scoreboard to tally gains and losses, no foreknowledge to cushion defeat and no suspicion to temper victory. Without it, they had no motor, no juice, no steam. No chance.

WHEN I WAS a young teenager, and black consciousness was rearranging all our heads—I must have been in the ninth grade at Felton at the time—some issue arose that galvanized me and my classmates into action. I don't remember what it was, and I'm sure that now it would seem utterly trivial—how we were allowed to wear our hair, what we'd be permitted to say at some upcoming school assembly—but at the time it was the most important thing in the world. Whatever position we were taking, for or against, was clearly the righteous one.

We did what everyone did in such circumstances in the sixties: We called a meeting. The only place we could meet was a second-floor room in a little white building that was owned by South Carolina State and stood across the railroad tracks from the campus, near the intersection that was known as Railroad Corner and just down the street from Trinity Church. It was barely a five-minute walk from my house.

We packed ourselves in, thirty or forty of us, and I remember there was lots of shouting and there were lots of raised fists and we kept trying to bring the anarchic conversation back to the subject of action, though we couldn't seem to decide on any. I'm almost positive that none was ultimately taken. I recall one image clearly, though: Gregory Daniels, who was one year behind me in school, rallying us with a Hendrix-style bandanna tied around his brow and a red-and-green-and-black Afro pick raised in his hand like an avenging sword.

Even then, I could see the irony. Greg was light-skinned and thought by all the girls to be devastatingly handsome. His hair was sandy brown and curly rather than kinky, soft and curly and fine. He had even less use for his pick than I had for mine, but there he was, waving it to make his point, conclusively demonstrating that despite the inconvenient fact of being the color of blond polished wood, he was actually as black as anybody in the room.

Our young anger grew out of color, but color seemed to be less a fact than a state of mind. Put another way: Our minds were black, therefore we were black. No matter what color we actually were, we *demanded* to be black.

In Brazil, most people with some measure of African blood demanded to be *not* thought of as black. In Brazil, most black people don't seem to feel themselves at all in conflict with white society. In Brazil, when a national newsmagazine did a celebratory cover on black success stories, the seventeen exemplars on the cover included one judge and a bunch of athletes and entertainers—not a single politician, businessman, writer, or scholar.

These things are connected.

After years of traveling around Brazil, I could see those connections clearly now. I could also see that the things about the race issue in America that had bothered me so much and helped drive me away—the obsessiveness about it, the choosing of sides, the discomfort, the paranoia, the anger—at worst had to be thought of as necessary evils, and perhaps even deserved to be called godsends. I still loved this fabulous new country I'd discovered and explored, but I was no longer under any illusion that it offered the answers that I once thought I'd found on the beach at Ipanema—no longer certain, in fact, that Brazil was even framing the question properly. I knew that both question and answer, at least for me, lay somewhere amid the tension and heartache and angst of the American struggle with race.

I also knew that many Brazilians, both black and white, would disagree violently with me; that they would say their way—without friction, without heat—was the better way to make the machine run. But I'd seen both approaches, and I'd seen the results. I saw that ignoring race didn't work any better than being obsessed about it, and I knew that in America, despite all our problems, I could put together a dozen magazine covers of black role models that included more than basketball players and soap opera stars.

Note that I said "our" problems. I was still half a world away, sleeping beneath the Southern Cross instead of the Big Dipper, but part of me was already home.

Chapter 10

Let the Church Say, "Amen!"

BRAZIL STILL TROUBLED ME, SO I DID WHAT MANY PEOPLE DO when they're troubled by the world: I went to church.

High on a hill in Salvador da Bahia, the historic city I first visited with Avis and Aaron on our tour of the country, stands a church named Nosso Senhor do Bonfim. It's a Catholic church, not surprisingly — Brazil is the most populous Catholic country in the world — but it has a second purpose as well. The church is also dedicated to Oxala, the most powerful of the Afro-Brazilian gods, collectively known as the *orixás*. N. S. do Bonfim is visited by some people who worship only the Judeo-Christian-Islamic God, and also by some people who worship only the *orixás*; but most of the people who come to the church manage, at least to some extent, to believe in both.

I'd come to Salvador to try to better understand Brazil's view of color, and found instead something I hadn't anticipated finding at all: a measure of identity. Not only that: a measure of *racial* identity. And not only that: a measure of racial identity that embraced *me*, that reflected my history, that gave me instruction on how to live my own life.

I had come to Salvador, and I ended up taking the first steps on a long road home.

IT'S HARD TO FULLY appreciate the scale of slavery in Brazil. Reliable numbers, as always, are hard to come by, but it's generally agreed that the millions of African slaves brought into Brazil far exceed the number brought into the United States, mocking the wildest dreams of even the most ambitious Old South plantation owner. It's also agreed that Brazilian slavery, like all slavery in the New World, was sickeningly cruel. The whipping of slaves was legal in Brazil until 1835; slavery itself wasn't abolished until 1888, a full generation after the end of the American Civil War.

Untold numbers of those slaves were brought into the country at Salvador. Black Americans who visit the city almost always feel an instant connection of some kind. It varies from person to person: Some hear Salvador's music and think of New Orleans, others meet the city's black intellectuals and think of New York. For some, it's like visiting Gorée Island in Senegal, the port from which so many African slaves are said to have sailed. The thick, sour breath of Salvador's bloody history seems to rise from the cobblestone streets and infuse the air, like steam rising after a summer rain.

For me, the connection was with Charleston, South Carolina. Charleston was the city where my great-grandfather, Major Fordham, was born, grew up, was married, and launched his career, before moving his family to Orangeburg. Like Charleston, Salvador is a fabled port. Like Charleston, it's a city of faded glory. Like Charleston, it's full of graceful old buildings and a kind of languorous, fetid charm. Like Charleston, it was a slave depot that represented for many thousands of people the literal gates of Hell.

We had distant relatives in Charleston when I was growing up, and we used to visit fairly regularly. I remember my parents' taking me one day to the old part of the city to see the slave auction house, where presumably a number of my forebears were sold in irons. It was a puny place, a building that looked too small and insignificant to have been the stage for such grand tragedy. I felt a combination of emotions I'd never felt before—disgust and anger, of course, but also something I hadn't expected: an unsuppressable measure of shame.

When Avis, Aaron, and I had come to Salvador we'd wandered the streets of the historic part of the city—the neighborhood is called Pelourinho, or "little pillory," referring to the whipping posts where slaves were publicly tortured—until we happened across a big, open, cobblestone plaza surrounded by colonial-era churches and houses. Immediately, without resort to the guidebook, I knew that this was the place where the slaves were bought and sold. I knew, because I felt that same precise mix of emotions, including the same measure of shame, that I'd felt in Charleston looking at the auction block.

And now, back in Salvador but alone this time, I went to Pelourinho and felt those emotions again. Where did the shame come from? I wasn't sure then, and I'm still not sure now, but it was unmistakable.

Pelourinho is full of churches, but everyone I talked to told me that N. S. do Bonfim was a special place, especially since I was in Salvador at the special time between Christmas and New Year's. So, even though it was far across town, that's where I went.

N. S. do Bonfim sits on a hilly peninsula far from the city center, its twin bell towers and golden cupolas overlooking the Bay of All Saints. The week after Christmas is the time when worshipers prepare for the most important festival of the calendar, which begins with the new year—the ritual washing of the church. It is a time of literal and metaphorical purification. By the thousands, people come to the church dressed all in white, repentant for the sins of the old year, prayerful for the promise of the new. They celebrate the birth of the infant Jesus, son of the Virgin Mary, and they also honor Oxalá, owner of the sun, the greatest of the Afro-Brazilian gods.

The *orixás* are a pantheon of West African deities imported on the slave ships that spilled their cargoes onto Salvador's docks. Try as they might, the slaveowners couldn't whip these gods out of the Africans' hearts and minds. The Catholic church couldn't exorcise them, despite many long years of effort. Now it no longer even tries, accepting this idolatry as the price that must be paid to keep the faithful coming in.

At one point in my life, when I was dutifully trooping with my family to Trinity church in Orangeburg every Sunday, I'd have called this blasphemy. At another point, during my days in Ann Arbor or San Francisco, I'd have been completely indifferent, or might even have ridiculed it as hocus-pocus. But now, in Salvador, I saw reflections of myself, felt vibrations of my own historic and cultural faith. For the first time in years, I saw and felt the power of the church—the *black* church. And to recognize that power I'd had to come all the way to Salvador, to a place where so many black people didn't even admit to being black.

I grew up going to Trinity every single Sunday, dressing to the nines, singing in the choir, fidgeting through the sermons. It was just another part of a fairly seamless childhood: Most of my friends went to Trinity too, and so I knelt at the communion rail with the same kids I'd see on the Felton playground the next day.

As soon as I left Orangeburg, though, I lapsed. Church-going had no place in my new life of freedom in Ann Arbor, certainly not at the beginning of the seventies, when belief in the Age of Aquarius was the only faith that seemed relevant. Something called "spirituality" was in fashion, however. I had a vague appreciation for a generalized, nonspecific notion of spirituality, whatever that meant, but little use for religion and no use at all for any church. The one exception was when I went home to Orangeburg to visit. I was obliged to sit in my old pew at Trinity, profess the old creeds, sing the old hymns—despite obviously being much too cool for such things.

I softened as I got older, of course, as everyone does. I was never antireligion, and when it came time to get married, there was never really any question of our being married anywhere but in a church. Avis was raised Catholic, and so we were married in her family's Catholic church. This meant that technically I was supposed to receive Catholic instruction; in point of fact this was far more than a mere technically, more like an absolute requirement. But the priest who married us—an old, liberal, Vatican II priest who believed in the spirit of church law rather than the letter—was satisfied to ascertain that I wasn't a complete heathen, that I'd been instructed in a recognized Christian faith, and that I could look him in the eye and promise to raise our children as Catholics.

We didn't actually go to church with any regularity until Aaron grew out of the toddler stage and we started to wonder, as parents do, about moral instruction: Precisely where was he supposed to get it, if not in a church? That, for better or worse, was where both of us had gotten it. So in Argentina, of all places, we eased back into the world of organized religion by starting to attend an ecumenical American community church. The pastor was Presbyterian but the congregation was from an assortment of Protestant faiths. For some reason, though, it was a real hotbed of church politics. Turned off by the cliques and the power plays, we shifted to the Catholic church near our house, actually a chapel in a convent where visiting priests offered Mass in English every Sunday. One good thing about the strict Catholic hierarchy is that church politicians need not apply—unless they are prepared to embrace celibacy and take vows. For Avis it was an intense and mixed experience, a problematic coming home to an institution that both comforted and exasperated her. For me it was a generally pleasant experience that probably meant a good deal less to me than it should. I had no stake in this church, no struggle with it. The truth is that as far as I was concerned, it wasn't much more than religious tourism.

At N. S. do Bonfim I was a literal tourist, at least at first. But not for long—not after I saw the women.

Amid the vast crowds of people, my eye was drawn to a group of about a dozen women who sat on the steps leading up to the church, selling incense and potions and food—ample, middle-aged black women, dressed head to toe in white. For a moment I wondered what was so shockingly familiar about them. Then it came to me: They looked just like the women who sat together in the front pews on communion Sundays at Trinity. Dressed head to toe in white, they helped prepare the sacrament and helped guide the parishioners to the rail, where we knelt and sipped sweet grape juice meant to represent the blood of Christ. These women in Brazil could have been the mothers and sisters and daughters of those women in South Carolina. The shock of recognition was so intense that I just stood there staring, and they must have thought I was either very rude or very simple.

The day had a soulful feel, a *black* feel, like a revival. I was tempted to think I'd finally found a black Brazilian setting, a setting that was black in the American sense of the word. But when I looked closer, I saw that it wasn't quite the same. Among the worshipers coming to the church were many whom I'd classify as white—in fact, the racial composition seemed about the same as that of the city as a whole. Poor black Brazilians came on foot or by bus; affluent white Brazilians arrived in their cars. But once they arrived they were all black, in a cultural sense. They joined together in ceremonies that were part medieval Europe, part ancient Africa.

So this wasn't quite like home, after all: White people didn't come to Trinity church, as a general rule. But their presence in respectable numbers at N. S. do Bonfim was a revelation that altered my vision of the place. Here were all these whites, participating in open, overt, heartfelt "blackness." The only way white people did "blackness" back home was by giving each other high-fives, listening to rhythm-and-blues and hip-hop and jazz, and appropriating snippets of black English, like "good to go." The worship I was seeing in Brazil clearly went much deeper.

And something else seemed to be at work, something familiar. The crowd was, after all, majority black. And yet this was Brazil, so I could be confident that many of those black people, perhaps even most of them, wouldn't even consider themselves black. And yet they all seemed to be supported and uplifted and propelled by this black Brazilian spirituality.

I was beginning to feel the power of this black church. And as I did, I also began to appreciate the power of the black church I'd left behind.

SALVADOR IS WHERE the African presence in Brazil began and where it remains most intense. It is also the place in Brazil where you are most likely to find people who have begun to perceive black consciousness and black identity not as a function of skin color, but more akin to the way we perceive it in America.

On a narrow street in Pelourinho there is an old colonial building whose doors are almost always open. Standing in that doorway as I walked past one day was Mauro, a copper-colored young man with sandy brown dreadlocks. He beckoned me inside.

"This is our cooperative," he said. "Come look at our art."

Inside was a wondrous jumble of pieces much finer than the tourist kitsch that lined the souvenir shops up and down the street. There were wood carvings of all the various Afro-Brazilian gods and goddesses, most prominent among them Yêmanjá, the mermaid goddess of the sea. There were carvings of an old black man smoking a pipe, a representation of a slave called the Preto Velho, or "Old Blackie," a figure that looked Uncle Tomish and submissive but that Mauro said represented revolution, at least to him. There were carved totems, rough hewn and unmistakably phallic, designed to ward off the evil eye. There were finely detailed paintings of street scenes, naive in their use of perspective and Caribbean in their use of bright, sun-splashed color, peopled with black women in dresses of billowy white lace standing in formal arrangement before colonial houses and baroque churches. And there were paintings of a more lurid, less representational style that seemed to convey pure emotion and re-minded me of Edvard Munch, a style that perhaps could be called Afro-Brazilian Expressionism.

Mauro had guessed that I was an American, and he seemed more interested in showing me the art and explaining it than convincing me to buy it. He introduced me to a couple of other artists who were at work in the studio, pointed out examples of his own work, and asked me about black artists in the United States. I stayed about a half-hour, browsing, chatting, talking about artists I admired in the States, answering questions.

"We are brothers," he said as I left. "Tell everyone in America that we are brothers. You are my brother."

That evening, I went down into a basement dance hall nearby to hear some live music. As was typical in Salvador, the crowd was all black except for a few French tourists. The music was percussive, insistent, hot. I finished my beer, and before I could buy another, a brown-skinned man standing next to me had offered me some of his. *"Irmão,"* he said, as he poured the beer. "Brother."

Salvador's population is overwhelmingly black. Just how overwhelmingly is a matter of some dispute, as naturally it would be in a country where more than half the people look black, at least to me, but only about 5 percent tell census takers that they're black. There's no question, though, that the percentage in Salvador has to be two-thirds, or three- quarters, or even more. Put another way, the number of Bahians who look white in the American sense is quite small.

In Pelourinho, virtually all the arts and crafts and music seemed to refer to the African diaspora in some way. The vendors and artists wore dreadlocks, dashikis, kente, tie-dye. Even the Salvadoran tourist caps and T-shirts were invariably red, green, and black, the colors of black liberation.

It all reminded me of the moment, around 1967 or so, when black suddenly became beautiful. I was thirteen that summer, just about to leave Felton to enter the tenth grade at Orangeburg High. Negroes were becoming black people before our very eyes, and our blackness—our color—suddenly was something to rally around in a way it hadn't been before.

The key to it all was to go out and buy an Afro pick.

The purest expression of the black-is-beautiful movement was the towering Afro, a celebration of Negritude and a rejection, finally, of pressing and dyeing and soaking with lye and all the other things that had been done over the centuries to perfectly good black hair to make it look more white. The Afro was an emblem of revolution, like a bandolier slung across a guerrilla's chest.

To my abject humiliation, I couldn't grow a proper one. Try as I might, my hair would get to a certain length—a length, I might add, far too short to shock or insult or even mildly annoy white American society; a length, in fact, that probably would have been perfectly acceptable on an ambitious young banker—and then it stopped growing. No amount of care and grooming, or at least no amount I had the patience for, would coax it into getting any longer.

But I could buy a pick, and I did. Carrying a pick with a red, green, and black handle sticking out of your back pocket was significant. It meant you didn't belong to the Negro generation that continued to fuss over its hair with fine-toothed combs and greasy pomades and stiff brushes. You were black, no matter what color your skin really was—and, no matter what the length or texture of your hair, it meant you saw it as an Afro. My pick had long metal tines that eventually shredded the back pocket of every pair of pants I owned. Using it, I raked my poor scalp like a vegetable plot at planting time. But it was worth the righteous pain. Every citizen soldier had to suffer for the revolution.

And revolution it was. To celebrate kinkiness of hair, a quality my parents and their parents had worked so hard to banish, was truly revolutionary. It was the most tangible and immediate manifestation of the fundamental change in our status, from being described as a race to being described as a color — embracing our newfound identity as black, black, black.

Salvador seemed, at least on the surface, to be in the midst of that kind of awakening. But the more I looked around, the more I saw that it really wasn't, at least not yet. Our awakening was about more than culture. It was, among other things, about wrestling away political power, and black people in Salvador had none; despite being a clear majority, they were not electing their candidates or even pushing their issues to the fore. It was about organizing to press for change, and black people in Salvador weren't really doing that in any substantive way. It was about confronting white society with demands, about getting in the nation's face and insisting on being seen and heard, and people in Salvador weren't doing that either.

Yet there was something at work in Salvador that partly compensated, something that seemed to hold black people together in a way I hadn't seen elsewhere in Brazil. It wasn't something of this world. It was spiritual, and it was powerful.

I began to understand it through Emiliano.

Emiliano Costa is a local entrepreneur with dark, dark skin the color of bittersweet chocolate. "Around midnight" might be the approximate label. There's never been any ambiguity in his mind, or in the mind of anyone who looked at him, even in ambiguous Brazil: For all of his nearly fifty years, he's been black.

Emiliano, whom I met by chance, became my guide to Salvador's heart and soul. He was intrigued at meeting a black American, and particularly insistent that I see the center and essence of black Brazil through the eyes of a black man.

Here, finally, was a black Brazilian who felt at least a measure of racial solidarity. One day, as we were threading our way through traffic in my hotel's posh beachside neighborhood, Emiliano cut off a young man who had to slam on his brakes and screech to a halt.

"Idiot!" the young man yelled.

"You're a queer, buddy," Emiliano yelled back.

Then he turned to me and grinned, happy with himself. "White people still think they own everything, that they even own the street," he said. "Well, they don't. You and I both know that they don't. Not anymore."

His antagonist might or might not have passed muster as white in America, but to Emiliano's way of thinking he clearly did, and he represented a class of people who seemed to believe they occupied society's heights by some sort of divine right.

Emiliano went on muttering, as we drove the curving coast road toward the heart of town, about how things were changing, how black people were rising up. I thought I heard real bitterness in his voice, the kind I'd heard back home for so many years in response to so many slights, insults, and indignities. It's a strange thing to be buoyed by hearing bitterness in someone's voice, but I was. I'd been wondering where the anger was in black Brazil that would finally begin to change things, where the rage was; and while this was really nothing more than grumbling, it was the closest I'd come to feeling I was in the presence of genuine black outrage.

But then suddenly it all dissipated.

"Look, there's the Spanish Club," he said, and a kind of boosterish pride had replaced the bitterness.

The Spanish Club was like an exclusive country club right next to the sea, with swimming pools and tennis courts, and also a stage where top-flight musicians like Caetano Veloso or Daniela Mercury regularly performed. Immediately, I noticed something I considered important about the people lounging around the pool and lunging across the tennis courts.

"The people there are all white," I said.

"Hmmmm. Yes," he said, as if noticing for the first time.

"Do any black people belong?"

"I don't know."

"Can they join? Could you join the Spanish Club?"

"Sure I could," he said, sounding a bit defensive. "I could be a member."

I let it drop, but the fact is that the only black people in evidence at the Spanish Club were the ones parking the cars and serving the drinks.

A minute later, Emiliano was lecturing about the dearth of black public officials, or at least black public officials who were willing to speak up for black people's interests—or even willing to acknowledge they were black at all. To hear Emiliano tell it, scores of mayors, deputies, and senators throughout Brazil were black, or at least dark enough to be considered one of the many shades of black, but didn't acknowledge this fact.

I thought that Emiliano, who was too dark to pass for anything except black, might resent these back-turning brothers. I certainly would have. But instead, he seemed to be speaking with a hint of pride. Together, these prominent people could make race a real issue in Brazil if they wanted to, but Emiliano didn't seem to mind that they preferred to consider themselves white. The fact that they were out there—silent, passing, not rocking any boats—was enough. He insisted that even President Fernando Henrique Cardoso, who has always been classified as white, should be more properly considered *moreno.*

"He's a brown president," Emiliano told me several times. "Brown. Brown. Not a white one."

I grinned, thinking of the accepted wisdom among many black people in America that Bill Clinton has a bit of black blood somewhere in his family tree. Just a drop or so—but one drop is enough in America. This explained why "they" were always after him, always trying to pull him down, and why "they" couldn't stand to see him succeed.

We swung inland through the commercial heart of the city, where the streets took on the feel of a Third World marketplace. In front of the stores and office buildings, a solid phalanx of vendors hawked knapsacks, lingerie, sunglasses, pots and pans, any manner of merchandise. The crowds here were almost exclusively black, at least to my eyes. The fanciest shopping centers and the newest office buildings were all on the periphery, miles away; this downtown, like so many other downtowns I had seen in so many other countries, was fading fast.

When we reached a square called Piety, Emiliano quickly locked the car doors. Long ago, the plaza had been effectively taken over by crack-smoking street kids who stuck up motorists to support their habits, threatening them with knives and guns through their car windows. The city couldn't be bothered to do anything for them or about them.

Emiliano plowed through the old part of the city and then beyond, to a bayside neighborhood called Ribeira. It was a depressed little community of run-down houses and rutted streets, but the unimpressive infrastructure was more than made up for by the setting: Ribeira was snuggled against a tight cove, where fishing boats pulled in and out to serve a local fish market and a string of seafood restaurants. These were popular joints, working-men's joints, that sold cheap, spicy food and big, ice-cold bottles of beer. On the waterfront, vendors offered samples of tropical fruits I'd never seen before in all my previous trips to Brazil, including one called *jaca,* an enormous thing like a soft-sculpture pineapple with firm, sticky flesh and a mild, almost melonlike taste. It was a slice of black Bahia, a kind of never-ending soul food picnic down by the dock of the bay, everything moving at its own pace, no tension, no rush. I could have spent the whole day right there.

But Emiliano wanted to take me farther inside, farther back, and so we piled back into the car and headed away from the waterfront. We drove through poor, ugly, dust-choked industrial zones, until we found the freeway that would take us to a place called Cachoeira—a journey to the interior, and also an interior journey.

The highway led through suburbs and past factories until it spilled out onto a vast plain and the farmlands began. This was the Brazil of the colonial plantations; this was where Brazilian slavery had first begun to flower.

The rich agricultural bottomland beyond the Bay of All Saints, an area called the Recôncavo, sustained the early Portuguese colonists and many generations of their descendants. With the help of the slaves they were busily importing, the colonists first grew sugarcane, and then when that trade began to fizzle they branched out into another crop, harder to grow but just as lucrative—tobacco. The town where we were headed, Cachoeira, was at the heart of the tobacco-growing region. For a time, early in the eighteenth century, tobacco from Cachoeira was considered among the best in the world.

Today, Cachoeira is still the jewel of the Recôncavo. But it's a tarnished jewel. The town boasts an amazing trove of colonial-era buildings, almost all of them strikingly graceful, almost all of them crumbling to sad dust; money for renovation either has run out or never arrived in the first place. "Cachoeira" means water-fall, but the waterfall in question was obliterated many years ago by a dam and a system of waterworks that supply metropolitan Salvador. Connecting Cachoeira with its sister town of São Felix across the river is an 1855 railroad bridge built by the British. It is used by trains, cars, and pedestrians in turn, with the rubber-wheeled vehicles forced to rattle and lurch their way across on a roadbed of ancient railroad ties. As Emiliano and I went over and back, I had to remind myself that the thing was the better part of a hundred and fifty years old and it hadn't fallen yet, although it seemed ready to do so at any moment.

Besides being a museum of colonial architecture, Cachoeira is also a renowned center of authentic Afro-Brazilian culture. This aspect of the place is what Emiliano wanted me to see.

We ate lunch at a restaurant near the river. The walls were covered, floor to ceiling, with bas relief wood carvings depicting the Afro-Brazilian *orixás:* there was Yêmanjá, emerging in all her serenity from the sea; there was Oxalá, the vastly powerful first among equals; here and there were all the others. Other carvings were depictions of slavery: men in shackles, men being whipped, men taking their revenge on cruel masters. There were what looked like carved portraits of specific individuals, perhaps family members of the artist. There were animals and geometric patterns and patches of what looked like pure design. And there were scenes that might have been novelistic and might have been allegorical: a panel, for example, that depicted a licentious drinking party, with one man passed out and another turning away from his wife to fall into the arms of a loose woman in high heels.

The racial mix in this sleepy Brazilian town, or rather the color mix, seemed about the same as in Salvador and the rest of Bahia. It was arguably darker, on average, but not markedly so. The feeling of the place, though, seemed markedly less European than the rest of the country that I'd seen, even less European than the most Afrocentric parts of Salvador. There was nothing contrived or political about this blackness; it seemed organic, rooted, somehow pure.

At the central market I bought some mangoes because they looked so perfect. Meanwhile, Emiliano fell into a long discussion with a wizened old man with one arm. After a while the old man set down the gym bag he was carrying and began rummaging through an assortment of plastic bags, which were stuffed with what looked like twigs and leaves and old soda bottles that had been refilled with liquids of various unnaturally bright colors. After considerable back-and-forth Emiliano bought a bag of twigs and a bottle of shocking green.

"This is good for the blood," he explained, showing me the twigs. The old man nodded and said you had to brew it, whatever it was, like a tea. "And this," Emiliano said, gesturing with the green juice, "is for the blood sugar. I have trouble with the blood sugar."

Emiliano was an educated man who went regularly to the doctor and had been told to avoid sugar. This he did, faithfully, as any prudent man would obey the considered advice of modern medicine. But he also found it prudent to drink a bottle of dirty-looking green stuff on the advice of an old man he'd never met before. I asked if he had any idea what was inside the bottle, and he just shrugged. The old man had said he was a healer, and he had seemed like a healer. He'd had the sense of a healer about him. If it didn't work, Emiliano said, he'd try something else.

We toured the city for a while, taking in the sights, but really we were just marking time until our appointment. We were going to see Mother Dionisia.

More than the talented artisans, more than the traditional healers, more than the old buildings, what gave Cachoeira its cachet were the dozens of priests, priestesses, seers, intermediaries, whatever you want to call the men and women who led the practice of the Afro-Brazilian cult religion usually known as *macumba* or *candomblé*. Mother Dionisia, by widespread reputation, was one of the most powerful.

I'd spent a bit of time back in Salvador trying to learn more about the religion, and even had visited the headquarters office in Pelourinho where the paperwork necessary to any organized church was handled. There, patient elders had tried to explain the essence of *candomblé* to me, but I hadn't really taken much in. Here in Cachoeira I hoped to get a better sense of what it was about.

We drove to a neighborhood on the outskirts of town, down by the river, then parked and climbed a staircase leading up a steep hillside to Mother Dionisia's compound, a string of improvised concrete-block structures that were the most solid and substantial in the area.

A wall-eyed young man in gym shorts and rubber sandals answered the door, looked us over, and led us to the *terreiro*, the place where the worship ceremonies actually took place. The walls of the *terreiro* were painted with pictures of the *orixás*, including a striking blonde Yêmanjá with the tail of a fish and a look of serenity on her androgynous face that recalled Botticelli. There we were kept cooling our heels for a half-hour.

When we were judged to have waited long enough, we were summoned to Dionisia's inner lair. Dionisia looked to be in her sixties, although she'd probably had a tough life, the kind of life that ages a face, and might have been younger. She was very dark, very stout, and wore a loose dress with a simple geometric pattern that looked vaguely West African. This was a high priestess who obviously didn't need elaborate vestments or other accoutrements of power; her authority and her mysticism were in her eyes, big dark piercing eyes that commanded attention and respect.

It was a tiny, windowless room. Candles burned, making the chamber much warmer than the rest of the house; the walls were covered with drawings and paintings of the *orixás* and written incantations. Dionisia sat at a table on which long strands of beads were arranged to form a rectangle. She was barefoot, and she made Emiliano and me take off our shoes as well. She looked me in the eye and told me with utter confidence that she was going to see my future.

Dionisia grabbed up a handful of cowrie shells that were piled in a corner of the table. She shook them, the way one might shake a pair of dice, and began to pray. Then she ordered me to pray as well.

I hesitated, and she fixed me with a stern look. It didn't matter what language or religion I chose, she said, but I had to pray. This was a powerful woman, full of authority and presence. I had come to observe and learn, not really to participate, but I found myself muttering the Lord's Prayer.

Dionisia tossed the shells into the rectangle formed by the beads and began to read the signs.

"You will have no great problems, no great problems," she said. "Your *orixás* are Oxalá and Yêmanjá, very powerful *orixás*. They will always protect you."

Again and again she tossed the shells, and each time they landed she evaluated the pattern they made and read the implications for my future. A tall man and a short man were conspiring against me at work, she said, and I should beware. A light-skinned woman, a temptress, was trying to seduce me, but I must not give in, because if I did, I would lose everything. I had two sons. My family would enjoy good health. My *orixás* were so powerful that in general I had very little to worry about, but there were two months in particular when I shouldn't travel.

No recounting could adequately capture the intimacy of the moment or the power this woman exerted, even over a foreigner who didn't even really understand what this faith was all about, let alone fully share it. There was something I shared with Dionisia, though, and it didn't depend on formal theology or even need words to find expression.

Some of her insights did fit the facts of my life, but that didn't quite seem to be the point. What mattered was that all of them were *real*, all of them genuine. That little room was filled with the power of faith, and I was overwhelmed by it. This was a poor woman who ministered to poor people; she was without money or connections, without influence in any traditional sense, and yet she had power. I'd witnessed a few black preachers in Baptist churches back home doing the same thing that she had done to me: She had cast a spell, she had brought me along with her on a journey, and in the process she had imparted some of her great strength to me.

Next it was Emiliano's turn.

Dionisia began just as she had begun with me, and then from that point on hardly was able to get a word in edgewise; as soon as she tossed the shells the first time, and observed that Emiliano was having some financial trouble, he began to spill out all his problems, all the many crosses he had to bear, all the injustices that were being visited on him in this manifestly unjust world.

His business was going well enough, he said, but the problem was his wife. A few years ago she had decided she wanted to open a school, one that would teach reading to young children. It was a noble cause, given the condition of public education in the country, and he had been supportive. Very supportive. She had needed money for the building, money for the supplies, money to pay the teachers, money for everything. There had never been enough students to begin to pay the costs, so the whole thing had started to go downhill. She had failed to pay one of the teachers, and the teacher had gone to court to sue for the money. Now he, Emiliano, was being held liable. Was this fair? And his wife still wouldn't close the school, although it was obvious it was a complete failure. And then there was his girlfriend, who was so immature, always wanting presents; and there were his children, who needed money for their schooling and everything else; and his health, you know, he hadn't been feeling that well lately. Did he look well? Was this the face of a healthy man?

It was a religious exercise but also a therapy session, and I realized that *candomblé* played a role analogous to that played by the Negro church in Jim Crow America. The world seemed unjust because it *was* unjust. Sometimes you had to escape from it, through transcendental ceremonies in the *terreiro* that featured hypnotic music and rhythmic chanting and that drew worshipers out of their earthly bodies, into a better place. Sometimes, though, rather than escape from the world, you needed to process it, to talk about it, to deal with it. Emiliano needed to talk to Mother Dionisia.

At the end she mixed him up a bag of what looked like lawn mulch, which was supposed to improve his health and right some of the wrongs in his life, and when he left he felt much better. He could take it along with the twigs and the shocking green he'd bought from the old one-armed man.

Dionisia offered, for a fee, to perform a more elaborate ceremony that would guarantee my future prosperity. The fee was so steep that I had to demur. She said that at least, then, I should make an offering to Yêmanjá before I left Brazil, to thank her for my good fortune and appeal for her continued protection. Typically, she said, this would be an offering of food, presented at the seashore.

I had reached across the many miles, across the yawning centuries, and touched ritual and belief that went all the way back to the West African village, the place from which my ancestors had been untimely ripped. What I'd found, though, was far from exotic—was, in fact, quite familiar. It was an affirmation of faith, of the spirit. This worship, available to all Brazilians, fundamentally belonged to black Brazil. I could see now that there was at least one thing that held black Brazilians together, that defined them, that offered refuge and shelter and strength to people desperately in need.

Emiliano arrives in his fancy car to visit Dionisia in a meager slum estate and learns wisdom that keeps him going for another few months. My father, with his learning and accomplishment, kneels at Trinity's rosewood rail next to a gardener who has worn the same shiny suit to church for as long as I can remember.

I had gone all the way to Brazil to see the essence of something that was right down the street all along.

In America, men and women much wiser than me had recognized the power of faith and used it as the focal point of the civil rights movement, from Ralph Abernathy to Martin Luther King, Jr., to Jesse Jackson to Louis Farrakhan. So far, in Brazil, that hadn't been done. But it was easy to see the potential, and easy to posit that the factor that kept Brazil's preachers and priestesses and seers from becoming leaders in the more political sense was precisely the factor that had seemed so attractive about Brazil at first, the absence of racial identification.

The Brazilian black church spreads its essence throughout the society: a lot of the supplicants at N. S. do Bonfim are white, as are many of the hundreds of thousands who gather on Rio's beaches each New Year's dressed in white to give praise to Yêmanjá. The black church in America, on the other hand, is exclusive by race, and this exclusivity has the effect of concentrating its power. The church functions like a glue to give African Americans more of a reason to believe in one another than they might have otherwise. It gives its worshipers comfort and guidance, but also shield and sword. It gives them — it gives *us* — a framework for needed action, not just in our private lives but in the public sphere as well. When my family and I drove the few blocks down Boulevard each Sunday to Trinity church, we weren't just doing something spiritual, we were also committing a political act, a social act, an act of self-love. I was beginning to see a power here that I'd never fully appreciated, a power that comes from faith, of course, but also from race, from identity. I found myself wishing that *macumba* and *candomblé* were more exclusive, that they were less welcoming, that they conserved and concentrated and focused their power to uplift the people — the black people — at the core of the faith.

When I got back to my hotel room in Salvador, I felt electrified. It wasn't until later that evening that I remembered I had a duty to fulfill. I grabbed one of the mangoes I'd bought at the market in Cachoeira, took the elevator down to the lobby, made my way through a crowd of French tourists, walked to the beach, and tossed the mango as far out to sea as I could. Into the arms of Yêmanjá.

Chapter 11

Triangulation

AFTER FOUR YEARS IN SOUTH AMERICA MY TOUR OF DUTY WAS UP. My editors were eager for me to take another posting, so I asked for something in the First World—something, say, in Europe. For a while it looked like Bonn was our most likely destination, which spurred Avis, Aaron, and me to begin taking German lessons from a teacher at the American school who'd been born near Munich. Fortunately for the German language, Bonn was a mere feint; my boss called one day and asked if maybe, possibly, I might be interested in London instead. It took me all of a nanosecond to accept.

Then I set out for one last reporting trip to Brazil.

The excuse was a big international conference in Rio, but my presence in the meeting hall wasn't so desperately needed. In truth, I mostly wanted to take a kind of farewell tour around the city. I'd fallen in love with Rio and then fallen out of love with it; the city had fired my imagination, with its promise of a new way of seeing and being, and then destroyed my illusions in the heat and frenzy of a night at the Sambadrome. Now, at the point of separation, Rio de Janeiro and I finally came to terms.

It was likely to be my last trip to Rio for some time, I knew, so I tried to partake of all the things I loved about the city—tried, in fact, to overdose on them. I always stayed on Copacabana Beach, and always spent hours walking up and down the esplanade, enjoying the sun and the sand and the nonstop entertainment of beachside life. This time, though, instead of my usual strolling back and forth, I took a whole afternoon to beach walk. I went all the way down Copacabana, with its funky, improvisational atmosphere, and then cut across to Ipanema and walked its length, too, enjoying the contrast—the farther I went, the more elegant the scene became, even though it's difficult to put into words exactly why one string bikini seems so much more elegant than another. Then I walked back to the hotel and kept going, all the way to the far end of the Copacabana strip, almost to Sugarloaf. A mountain blocked my way, definitively, so I turned back and went back to my room.

With Mac and a couple of other journalist friends, I went down to a restaurant near his office to eat a middling lunch, drink ice-cold beer, and tell old stories about our adventures in the Amazon, the favelas, and other haunts of Brazilian wildlife. The restaurant looked out onto Botafogo Bay, which had its own small private beach, a neighborhood beach where I never saw a single tourist. Barefoot, brown-skinned boys splashed in the water, playing tag. Another evening, we moved our feast to a fancy Italian restaurant. Our party, eight or ten strong, made so much noise that in any other country we might have been thrown out. But this was Brazil, a nation that abhors silence, and so in comparison with the other tables we were relatively subdued.

As I went around the city, I tried not just to behold all the breathtaking views but to examine them, really see them and sketch them in my mind: Christ the Redeemer with his arms extended, Sugarloaf standing sentinel at the entrance of Guanabara Bay, lush steep green hills behind gleaming white buildings behind blue water whipped with foam. It was truly the most beautiful city I'd ever seen. I tried to really hear the sidewalk musicians pounding their drums, really appreciate the utter perfection of the weather and the sea and the perfect bodies sprawled on the white sands of the beachs. I wanted to imprint these things on my mind so I would have them forever.

I had only two nights left when I saw the ad in the paper and realized I would have one last Brazilian experience to cling to: Antonio Carlos Jobim was performing in concert at an auditorium barely a five-minute cab ride from my hotel.

Jobim, of course, was the most famous Brazilian musician of all time, composer of some of the century's most sophisticated and infectious popular music. His best-known tune was "The Girl from Ipanema" (which sounds a lot better and less lounge-lizard-like in Portuguese than English), but he also wrote scores of other songs whose simple melodies and complicated rhythms were altogether unforgettable. Jobim was considered a national treasure, a living expression of the soul and spirit of Brazil. There were other Brazilian musicians whose work I enjoyed more because it was more contemporary, but none who approached his iconic status — and, probably, none whom history would so honor. I'd never seen him perform, and this might be my last chance. A no-brainer.

I went with a motley assortment of journalist friends and new acquaintances from the conference I was covering, including, I recall, two Aboriginal women from Australia. The truth is, I don't remember the precise composition of our group, and it doesn't really matter anyway. It was as if the only people in the whole vast auditorium were Tom Jobim and me.

He sat at the piano, of course, surrounded by a first-class band and three or four female singers. He was short and a bit pudgy, his face splotched and lined by a lifetime of drink and late nights and fevered creation. His voice was sandpaper and gravel, and had to work to carry those fabulous tunes. But the music, the history, the whole experience just lifted my heart. He played all his classic songs — "The Waters of March," "Felicidade," "Corcovado"—and they were no less fresh for being so familar. As a singer and even as a presence on stage, his best days were clearly behind him. This wasn't remotely his best performance. But still I was transfixed.

About midway through the show, I looked around at the audience for the first time, and I saw Brazil. There was a mix of skin colors, a mix of hair textures, a mix of body styles. Contrasting couples held hands and swayed to the familiar bossa nova beat, singing out the lyrics that everyone knew by heart. This was the Brazil I preferred to remember, the Brazil in which people of all races can sit and sing together in an atmosphere completely devoid of racial tension simply because they don't completely accept the concept of race.

Outside, at the end of a magical evening, lay the other Brazil. On the way back to the hotel I passed a group of street kids sleeping in a little park near the beach. It was a chilly night for Rio, and they were huddled in tattered old blankets. They were thin almost to the point of emaciation, their little bodies nourished only by what they could scavenge or steal. All the kids were black. The people in fancy cars driving past, and averting their eyes, were white. The society was able to ignore those facts, but I wasn't.

The next morning, I got on a plane and left Rio for the last time.

After a blurred few months of back-and-forth across the Atlantic, we arrived for good in London and our family settled into a wondrous Victorian pile in Hampstead, not a hundred yards from the Heath. The house, with its four floors and its ostentatious central skylight, was on an idyllic oval called Gainsborough Gardens, so cleverly tucked away that even a fair percentage of London's famously skilled cab drivers couldn't find it unless you gave them careful directions. We enrolled Aaron in a British prep school called The Hall that turned out to be an excellent school but a bit of a culture shock after our time in South America. Aaron wore a uniform each day; he went to Anglican chapel regularly; he was required to respond to authority in a manner that I found almost pathological; and he once was given a detention for dunking a basketball on the playground, because that simply was not "the way the basket is supposed to be used."

As for Lowell, we sent him to a nursery school over in Highgate, a school where the teachers were all young women who happened to be from east London. Almost immediately, he began to develop a charming Cockney accent.

After our time in Buenos Aires, after four years of being stared at every time we stepped out our front door, it was an absolute liberation to walk the streets of a city where nobody gave any of us a second look. And why should they? London is nothing if not cosmopolitan, full of people of every conceivable description. To attract the kind of attention on Oxford Street or Picadilly that we'd routinely attracted in B.A., we would have had to take off all our clothes and set fire to our hair. London is about the same size as Buenos Aires, but in the one city we'd been absurdly conspicuous and now in the other we enjoyed a welcome anonymity.

In other words, there were black folks in London.

Black people were visible on the streets, in the shops, in just about all parts of town. From the moment I arrived I had the sense there were a lot of them—of us—but I never really grasped how many until I set out to get myself and my sons competent haircuts.

The commercial sector in Hampstead included a first-class butcher, an adequate baker, and various sellers, if not makers, of candlesticks; there was a Valhalla of a bookstore and several restaurants that approached Nirvana; there was a curry shop and a cobbler and all that anyone could desire, but there was no barber, no hair salon that was equipped, either in terms of personnel or tools, to cut African hair. With the boys and me looking shaggier and more disreputable by the day, I finally piled Aaron and Lowell into the Underground and rode all the way down to the neighborhood called Brixton, the black metropolis on the other side of the Thames.

We emerged into the light from the Brixton station, and if not for the weather we could have been in some Caribbean or African outpost of empire. Reggae music blared from giant speakers outside a record store; two competing sidewalk preachers thundered their differing versions of salvation and damnation; strong voices sang in laughter. The clear majority of people on the crowded, jumbled, vibrant street were black.

I had vague directions to a barbershop: Turn left and then quickly left again; walk the length of the outdoor market, with its heaped fruits and vegetables, its tables of cheap clothes and cosmetics, its bootlegged music cassettes and videotapes; turn right, giving wide berth to the crack and hashish dealers who some-times hung out on the corner; look across the street, it should be around there somewhere.

It was—a tiny barbershop run by an affable, amply skilled, middle-aged gentleman from Jamaica whose name I never caught because I didn't understand a word he said.

This was no place to speak the queen's English. The barber shop was an Afro-Caribbean sanctuary, where black men gath-ered, exclusively, shut up cozily for a while against the cold, white world of England. Since the clientele was mostly Jamaican, the lingua franca was Jamaican patois, which meant that it wasn't re-ally franca at all, since Africans came in too, and of course we Americans, and none of us had a clue what was being said.

The barber would turn to a customer—someone like the jolly gray-haired old man who was there so often I thought for a while he was one of the barbers, except that he never cut anybody's hair—and say something that sounded like "hummana yummana hummana yummana an' all dat t'ing, mon." The old man would laugh, or nod solemnly, and respond with his own string of ran-dom syllables. My boys and I were mystified and amused.

Sometimes these perorations would be addressed to me, and I'd have to guess from the context whether to nod, shake my head, laugh, or tell the barber how much to take of the top.

The little that I could understand of the conversation inside the barbershop was familiar, and I found it reassuring, although at first I didn't understand why. The men who came in talked about sports—specifically, about Ian Wright, the black soccer player who was scoring goals at an amazing clip for his team, Ar-senal. They talked about show business—about Lenny Henry, the black comedian whose new television show was getting mixed reviews. They talked about women—about Naomi Campbell, the gorgeous model. They talked about the same things black men would talk about in a barbershop in Cleveland or Atlanta, about the achievements and foibles of black people who had in various ways distinguished themselves in the white world.

I started going to Brixton pretty regularly, and those trips gave me a new appreciation for the barbershop as an institution in all corners of what people now call the African Diaspora. I'd been unplugged for four years—in Argentina, with no alternative available, Avis had had to cut our hair. Now, sitting in that tiny shop, the smell of familiar pomades and liniments had an almost Proustian effect. I was transported to lost times; back to Mr. Middleton's barber chair in Orangeburg; back to Mr. Brunson's chair in the years after Mr. Middleton quit barbering and got into real estate and politics; back to Mr. Moore's barber chair on Lee Highway in Arlington; back to all the places I'd been clipped and trimmed and shorn, and been given an hour of inviolate sanctuary.

It was important to me, I realized, that there existed a place where black men gathered more or less exclusively, though there would be the occasional black woman having her short Afro trimmed or the occasional white guy wanting a fade like the black guys on his basketball team. The barbershop was clearly a black man's world. It had something to do with the need for refuge and something to do with the need for reinforcement. You could put down all the baggage for a while and gain strength so that when you picked it up again and walked out the door you'd be that much stronger.

Even in the most violent of America's urban war zones, the barbershop was a kind of demilitarized zone, the only place where a middle-aged banker would sit for an hour with a peach-fuzzed gangster on one side and a burly ex-con on the other and peace would reign. There was still etiquette in the barbershop: conversational subjects to be avoided, a strict first-come-first-served order for admission to the chair, an implied duty to share the magazines and make room in the waiting chairs. Even the baby gangsters dropped their blank stares and meekly followed the rules.

One of the most shocking murders recently in Washington, a city not easily shocked by murder of any kind, took place at a barbershop. A man lost a quarter in the pay phone, pulled a gun, and demanded that the barber refund it; the barber gave him the quarter, but the man shot him anyway. The city was outraged; *I* was outraged. It was a violation, a crime against decency and the rules of civilization, like storming into a medieval church to drag out an accused thief. It wasn't done. It was a crime against an important pillar of civilization, and thus it was a crime against us all.

It was a black thing. Not a universal thing, not a multicultural thing, a black thing. After years and years I was once again into black things.

WE SPENT JUST two years in Britain. In some respects it was a kind of halfway house between the exotica of South America and the prosaism of the United States, a cultural stepping-stone toward home. But it served another purpose as well: It was a place where I could triangulate the very different experiences I'd had of race, the better to pinpoint my own location on that complicated landscape.

The accepted official term for black people in Britain was "Afro-Caribbean," an awkward word that served two purposes. It distinguished between people of African heritage and others the British also considered "black," like Indians, Pakistanis,

Bengalis, most Arabs, and practically anyone else with a sun-
tan. And the term also emphasized the fact that black people in
Britain came from elsewhere,and in a sense still belonged to
elsewhere. For many, the phrase "black Briton" came haltingly,
if at all.

Still, however imperfect the nomenclature, the phenomenon
of black Britain clearly was elaborating itself day by day. The impact of black people on the culture was beginning to be felt in
fields other than athletics and entertainment, though not to any
great extent in politics. Calls for black pride and against racism
were beginning to echo. Black characters were turning up in nov-
els and television sitcoms about daily British life. Black people
had begun to invade the national consciousness.

I was aware of this encroachment partly because I was a
journalist and tried to pay attention to the society in an analytical
way. But even if I hadn't been, I'd have noticed what to me was
the most striking example of the way black people were entering
British society: the profusion of interracial couples I saw in the
streets and shops and restaurants of London.

Black men with white women; black women with white men.
The couples strolled hand-in-hand down New Bond Street,
canoodled on the lawns at Kensington Palace, strolled their beige
babies down the streets of Islington, emerged together from the
eateries of Covent Garden. I knew that it was perfectly normal
for people of all shapes, sizes, and colors to fall in love. I thought
it wrong, somehow, to notice — I even tried my best not to notice.
But notice them I did.

Triangulation:

In Brazil, it had been utterly commonplace to see differently
colored couples in most settings, except at the very highest
reaches of income and power, where there were only whites. But

these black-white couples were devoid of any larger visual impact, at least for my eyes, because there was no real racial context. In America, by contrast, interracial couples still packed a visual punch. Even if it were, say, a dark-haired woman of Italian descent walking hand-in-hand with a light-skinned black man, the distinction between their skin tones a mere matter of shadow and cast, the couple still made a statement.

Was there any good reason to allow the politics of race to extend so far into our intimate lives? Intellectually, I believed it was not. I still believe that love can be colorblind, even if justice has a harder time attaining that state; I still believe that love is love is love, and that love of any kind is better than its absence.

Yet when I married, I married a black woman. When we adopted a child, we adopted a black child. Actions do speak louder than words.

NOT LONG AFTER I arrived in London, a news story drew me to Manchester, the city where the Industrial Revolution had first flowered, and where I got to see another side of Britain—and another side of myself.

A killing had taken place in one of Manchester's largest housing "estates," a word that conjures images of manor houses and rolling meadows but really means "the projects." It was a gray, gritty, grimy place, all brick and concrete and bare earth. The dwellings were little townhouse-style units, jammed together along monotonous identical lanes and fronted by an unbroken string of dilapidated cars. Police cars cruised up and down the streets, playing cat-and-mouse with BMWs and Mercedes that I assumed belonged to drug dealers. This estate was a ghetto, plain and simple.

People in ghettos don't warm quickly to outsiders, and I wasn't having any luck trying to talk to passersby on the street. So I ducked into a little Jamaican carry-out, where I hoped I'd find people more relaxed and more willing to talk. Inside I found the reflection and echo of empire: There were a couple of middle-aged West Indian men chewing the fat, a couple of youngsters who might have been Hong Kong Chinese, and the man behind the counter, the one making up the Jamaican meat patties, was Pakistani. None of them was particularly eager to talk either.

I spent most of the rest of the day cruising around the neighborhood in my rented car. I saw a lot of minorities, a lot of immigrants, a lot of black and brown and yellow people—a lot of misery, a lot of hopelessness. It was a gray Manchester day, and this was one of the grimmest living environments, all in all, that I'd ever seen.

It took a while to dawn on me that there were others I hadn't seen at first, others more numerous than the blacks and the browns and the yellows, others who gradually came into focus as they strolled their out-of-wedlock babies, as they lurked to buy their illegal drugs, as they hid behind their threadbare curtains from the violence of the street. Most of the people in this desperate neighborhood, I slowly realized, were white.

I should not have been surprised by this; Britain is well over 90 percent white, and the majority in any setting is almost certain to be white. But I wondered why I hadn't noticed them on the Manchester estate, and why I had seen the blacks and the browns and the yellows instead.

Thinking back to the favelas of Rio and São Paulo and Salvador, I realized that I had looked at a milieu that Brazilians thought raceless and I had seen race—*black* people at the bottom of society's barrel. It was a clear, accurate view; I was sure of it.

But here in Manchester, where most of the people at the bottom were white, it had been a struggle for me to see the truth. Something had conditioned me to have that blind spot—something I'd absorbed in America.

I realized that throughout my whole life, I had been accustomed to seeing the worst, most intractable societal problems illustrated through the example of black people. I was, in fact, inured to it, to the point that I hardly even noticed it anymore. Journalists, academics, politicians, preachers, everyone with any kind of soapbox showed the same knee-jerk reflex: To explore a societal ill, the first thing to do was to head straight for the inner city and start poking and probing the black people who lived there. Want to do a television documentary about drug abuse? It's virtually impossible to catch suburban soccer moms in the act as they down handfuls of prescription pills, but it's a snap to stake out a streetcorner drug market and wait for the crackheads to file past at feeding time. Convinced that welfare is a ripe topic for a doctoral dissertation? No need to take the time and effort to venture all the way out to Appalachia or down to the bayous of Louisiana when the nearest large population of welfare recipients is just a ten-dollar cab ride from campus, in a neighborhood called Roxbury or Hunters Point or Bed-Stuy. Is teen pregnancy the Scourge-of-the-Day? Well, it's a good story however you tell it, but best of all if it's spiced up with the babies-raising-babies welfare-dependency absent-father scenario so easily found in the housing projects.

This reflex to put a black face on a problem is so strong and so widely shared that at some point I simply stopped noticing it and just accepted the premise that it implies, namely that "black people" equal "a problem." Eventually, through repetition, that idea becomes deeply imbedded and begins to affect everyone's perception of everything. You see a person with dark skin and you automatically assume some sort of pathology.

Once, when I was living in San Francisco, I went home to Orangeburg on vacation and took a camera with me. I wanted to try to capture some of the amazing visual scenes that I had grown up with. I spent a good deal of time down around Sunnyside, taking pictures of the tin-roofed shacks that still lined the unpaved alleys, weathered shacks perched on frail-looking pillars of bricks. There was one house in particular that I photographed again and again—I must have had a dozen exposures of this house, just the house without people, a portrait of desperate poverty in the South.

When I got back to San Francisco, I showed the pictures to a group of friends who happened to be white. One woman whom I'd known fairly well for several years was especially fascinated with the shots of that one house. She looked at all the exposures several times, and finally asked, in the sweetest innocence, "Is this *your* house, Eugene?"

My jaw dropped. I pulled out a photo of my own house, the graceful and commodious house that Major J. H. Fordham had built for his family, and waited for her to say something in apology, but no apology ever came—she just looked at the picture of my house, nodded, and went on browsing through the exposures I'd taken down in Sunnyside.

This was a woman who had had an upper-middle-class upbringing in the New York suburbs, her father a successful business executive. I'd been able to surmise that much about her upbringing within five minutes of our being introduced. What I hadn't realized was that she had sized me up in the same way—and she had seen poverty, problems, pathology. She had seen a black person.

And the thing is, I didn't even get mad at her. Not really. I was hurt, I was offended, but I didn't work up a real head of steam. It would be one thing if I'd repressed my rage, but the truth was that there wasn't anything to repress. I suppose I must have thought there was something understandable in her mistake.

Now, in Manchester, I was angry at myself. I felt guilty of a kind of self-hatred—and I vowed that this was a crime I would never commit again.

WHILE WE LIVED in Buenos Aires we were friends with a black British couple named Luke and Liz. He was an expatriate corporate warrior, like so many others in our gilded English-language ghetto; she was a nurse. They were roughly our age, and they had one child, a son who was a year or two older than Aaron. They were nice people, and while we didn't spend all that much time together, we shared the isolation of being black in a huge city where everybody else was white, and that fact alone made us close.

They left B.A. before we did—Luke was transferred home to London. When I learned we'd be coming to London as well, I called them. They were doing fine, Luke said, but life at home could be hard at times. There was so much racism to deal with, he said, there were so many hassles. There was a slight pessimism in his voice that I hadn't heard before, but I figured that anyone who'd just left the luxury and ease of life in Buenos Aires on the expatriate dole, and returned to the office politics and mortgage payments of ordinary life, would have to suffer a necessary period of adjustment. I chalked it up to culture shock. Luke seemed genuinely happy that we were coming, and he made me promise that as soon as we arrived we'd look them up.

It took us a few weeks to get settled, but we did call, and Luke and Liz invited us to their house for dinner. When we got there, the conversation naturally turned to what it was like to be black in London, and Luke and Liz warmed to the subject. There were lots of problems in all walks of life, they agreed, but especially in the workplace. The workplace, in fact, was very much on their minds these days.

Luke was having trouble at his job and might have to leave. He'd already begun to look for another, but with no luck so far. This he chalked up largely to his race.

"They're always very nice to you on the telephone when you're answering the advert," Luke said. "But then when you turn up for the interview, they take one look and they seem to lose interest."

I thought of Brazil, and of how many times that same thing must have happened to black men seeking employment. I assumed it was something that took place more or less constantly, given the racial demographics that were obvious in the Brazilian workplace—the lily-white corporations and lawyers' offices in the middle of a country full of black and brown people. After *carnaval* and my awakening to the unacknowledged role that race played in Brazil, there wasn't any way I could accept that kind of de facto economic apartheid as a coincidence. Yet I'd never heard a Brazilian man complain forthrightly, in such definitive terms, about being denied a job because of race. That meant, I supposed, that black Brazilian men in general might tend to be more satisfied with, and more confident of, their positions in society. But it also quite obviously meant that they were less likely to press for jobs on the basis of having been systematically denied opportunities that others—*white* others—in the society enjoyed. And it also obviously meant, given what I'd seen, that they were less likely to get those jobs.

In Brazil, the prevailing view was that class was in the end a much more powerful factor than race—class in the sense of wealth or its absence. It was class, not race, that confined people to the favelas, the national mythology held; class, not race, that won or lost good jobs. The poor, who were the majority, missed out, while the middle-class and the wealthy, who were a tiny minority, made out. Whatever impact race and color might have had was supposedly overwhelmed by the much greater impact of class.

But this just didn't seem to me to be true. Luke was educated, cultured, ambitious, talented; he was having trouble climbing as high on the ladder of British society as he was sure he could and should reach, but he didn't doubt his ability to get to those heights or his right to be there. I'd met black men and women of equal talents in Brazil, or at least of equal potential. But they'd seemed much more resigned to their status—because of class, or some other circumstance, or whatever. I just couldn't bring myself to see resignation as the correct response.

We talked well into the night. Liz was a nurse, which meant that her skills were in constant demand and she could always find work. But she was having to work huge amounts of overtime in order for the family to make ends meet, especially since the state of the local public schools was such that they found it necessary to send their son to a costly private school. That was to be his way higher up the ladder.

There was a kind of universality to the conversation: black people talking about the injustices of the white world in which they lived. Everything we said and heard that evening we'd said and heard before, talking to striving black couples in Washington or San Francisco or Orangeburg or wherever. These were things we'd all been through, at one time or another and in one way or another, and shared experiences go a long way toward forging a common bond. I remember the evening because it was an experience I had never had in Brazil, or anywhere else in South America. It was like being back in black America.

Black America: a place, and a state of mind, to which I was about to return.

Chapter 12

Reconnection

IT'S A HOARY CLICHÉ: THE TRAVELER RETURNS HOME AFTER A
lengthy sojourn abroad and finds himself in a changed land. On
reflection, he's forced to ask whether it's his homeland that's really
different, or whether he himself has undergone some metamor-
phosis he doesn't yet quite understand.

Well, clichés do happen.

Avis, the boys, and I resumed our American lives by reoccu-
pying our house in Tara. In our absence, the neighborhood had
changed. We were still the only black family, but many of the
houses had new occupants—young families with children, as opposed to the solid row of retirees we'd left behind. The older folks
who'd held on were, by and large, the right ones. There was much
less of an Old Dominion feel to the place, and this dampened the
culture shock just a bit.

Still, the shock was intense. The country we were reentering was a different place, and I was trying to reenter it on a different basis: older, more experienced, even a bit wiser, and certainly with a different perspective on the whole issue of race.

I was much more inclined than I had been in years to participate actively in the group labeled "black." That was my choice. But without choosing, I also was an automatic member of the special subgroup "black male," as were my sons. This took some readjustment.

I have always hated that phrase. In the first place, it is a homonym for "blackmail," which lends a certain negative connotation. Second, "male" is more naturally used as an adjective, not a noun. Animals and electrical plugs are male and female; when we talk about people we call them men and women. Even before I'd gone overseas, when I edited stories I always changed "black males" to "black men," and of course also made "black females" read "black women." I was like King Canute, though; the usage had overwhelmed my puny efforts and was by now firmly established in the lexicon.

And in my years in South America and Europe, the situation of black men in the United States had been deemed to reach such crisis proportions that the phrase "black male" was now not only standard but ubiquitous. That was the specific phrase used to describe a specific pathology with which the nation seemed wholly fascinated. In context, nothing else had a sufficiently clinical ring. Gradually I became almost numb to it.

Black men were in trouble when I left, it was widely agreed. When I got back, at least from what I read and heard, we seemed to be well past the trouble stage and fast on our way to eternal damnation.

My absence from the country had coincided with several ominous developments. As the black middle-class and working-class poured out of America's cities, those left behind found themselves with fewer and fewer economic prospects. The schools got worse, though I hadn't thought that possible. Jobs that paid anything resembling a living wage became even scarcer, though I hadn't thought that possible either. It simply wasn't possible for a poor young black man who had received limited parenting from a single mother and limited education from dysfunctional schools to enter the work force and find a legitimate job that paid him enough to live reasonably well. Such jobs just didn't exist. The economy has been changing for many years, but somehow in my years overseas its transformation had become complete. If you were poor and black and without skills, you had no place to go.

Into this hopeless situation came crack cocaine, and with it the crack economy. I agree with the economists that human beings are rational economic actors, and if ever any proof were needed, the example of the crack economy more than suffices. Given the situation it was perfectly rational for a young black man in the inner-city neighborhoods of Washington—or Newark, or Atlanta, or any other city for that matter—to launch a career in the crack trade. Unless he wanted to make minimum wage flipping hamburgers, crack was the one growth industry within this young man's limited horizons. It was the one industry that was always hiring. By standing on the right corner and being sufficiently clever in sizing up customers and competitors he could make enough money to keep his mother's electricity turned on, to buy food, to buy clothes and maybe even a car, to keep his baby son or daughter in diapers and the baby's mother in groceries. How else was he going to earn that kind of money?

The crack business had two major occupational hazards. One was violent death in a hail of gunfire, and this happened often enough for the statisticians to morbidly announce that homicide was the leading cause of death of such-and-such age group among "black males." The other hazard was arrest and incarceration. In a frenzy of antidrug zeal jurisdictions around the country passed draconian laws calling for mandatory imprisonment of anyone caught with more than a smidgen of crack, which happened to be a drug used overwhelmingly by black people and other minorities. Similar punishments were pointedly not mandated for those caught with powder cocaine, which happened to be a drug used overwhelmingly by white people who had too much money for their own good. Whether this was the intent or not, black men were locked up by the hundreds of thousands, by the millions, in numbers that were absolutely unprecedented. In some neighborhoods of Washington a sabbatical at Lorton prison in the Virginia suburbs had become almost a normal rite of passage, a kind of hard-edged version of summer camp. So many young black men were being arrested and sent away to prison because of these laws that the statisticians had to work overtime to calculate how much more likely it was that a given "black male" would go to prison than go to college.

The fact was, of course, that the vast majority of black men in America were neither murder victims nor murderers, neither crackheads nor crack dealers. But enough did fit into these categories that the phenomenon had become impossible to ignore. When I got back home I felt pressure from two sides. I felt that by virtue of my sex and my color I was automatically under suspicion—nothing really specific, just a general cloud of suspicion. At the same time I felt that I must be failing to meet some responsibility to make the situation better. I was a black man who was doing reasonably well. Wasn't it my responsibility to bring others along, to pull others out of that economic and moral swamp in which the most logical thing to do was carry guns and sell poison?

What I realized, coming home after those years away, was that as a black man in America, I was not really allowed to live a private life. At least that's how I felt. It was as if we were all on stage, living in public every hour of every day. Even in Argentina, where I stood out like a sore thumb, I'd felt more anonymous than I felt here at home. In the cafés of Buenos Aires, or in the middle of the Amazon jungle, or in my favorite barbershop in south London I'd felt as if I were being taken more or less at face value by the people I encountered. In America, to quote the old Black Panther line, I felt I was constantly being seen either as part of the solution or part of the problem.

My group had been judged the most troubled in our society. If I screwed up somehow, then I was just another statistic, just another contributor to the awful pathology of the "black male." Failure could never be personal; it would be a contributing factor in the collective failure of my group. If I managed not to screw up, then fine, but everybody would be watching, all the time, to make sure I never slipped. One stumble, and, well, there you see it, tsk tsk, another example of the inability of the black man to function properly in our society.

I became morbidly fascinated with the case of Joseph Jett, a young black Wall Street trader who had racked up record profits and been anointed a financial genius—and then had been fired, sued, and hauled before the federal authorities for allegedly faking all the profits, and thus inflating his own bonus, with smoke and mirrors. He maintained his innocence and said that his supervisors had been aware of every move he had made.

It was the press coverage of the case that I found so interesting. Having been a journalist for two decades I knew how chaotic and unfocused newsrooms always were—meaning that I knew with all my heart that "press conspiracies" simply didn't exist.

But why, in all the stories about Jett, did the major papers—including my own—seem to go out of their way to remind readers that he was black? Why did the long profiles that charted his rise and fall always mention telling little details like his elegant and expensive wardrobe, or the computer file that someone allegedly found in which he was said to have detailed his sexual conquests? If you did a survey I'm sure you'd find that most twenty something Wall Street millionaires, of any race, tend to dress expensively, since that's what's expected on the trading floors and they can afford it. Likewise, you'd find that most of them attract the opposite sex like flies, since youth and wealth are the greatest aphrodisiac combination ever devised. So why highlight these generic factors in writing about Joe Jett?

It was those same old assumptions again, the ones I'd fled to South America to escape. He wasn't just a "young rogue trader," he was a "young black rogue trader." Joe Jett, a nerdy little math whiz, had become a combination of Fancy Dan and Mandingo.

I was home.

AT LEAST I WAS fairly well equipped to deal with this kind of scrutiny, and so was Avis. My most immediate and intense concern was about what being back in America would do to our sons.

On the one hand, Aaron and Lowell would get to see their extended family a lot more often, and that could only be good for them. Our visits home from abroad had assumed a standard form—a flight to Washington, a week or so with Avis's family, a flight or drive to South Carolina, a week or so with my family, maybe a few days alone in the sun for Avis and me, and then back overseas. The boys and the families were both shortchanged. Avis's family compound outside Washington fairly teemed with nieces and nephews of all ages, who formed a crucial lifeline for Aaron and Lowell, giving them a sense of stability and continuity. For my parents, our boys were the only grandchildren, and as such were in constant demand. On every visit we'd have to go through two separate teary farewells.

We had also thought it important during our time overseas for the boys to have some ongoing connection to their own national culture, and this was hard to maintain with such brief and episodic exposure. Aaron had grown up playing soccer, for example, but perhaps out of the need to assert his Americanness had also become absorbed by baseball. Our visits home were our only chance to take him to a real big league ballgame, so we always made time for a visit to see the Baltimore Orioles play at Camden Yards. Similarly, as he got older, his trips home were his chance to see what kids were wearing, hear what music they were listening to, watch the popular television shows, and test all the new video games that would take months to reach even London, to say nothing of Buenos Aires.

The visits also had been their only real chance to spend time among other African-American children and absorb more intangible cultural influences. It was a way for Aaron to learn how to wear his pants sufficiently low on his hips, but not so low that they fell off. It was a way for Lowell to begin to lose the mild Cockney accent he'd picked up from the East End girls who took care of him at his London nursery school. All this was important: We didn't want them to come back as clueless as a couple of extraterrestrials.

But now that they were back, and once again enrolled in American society, I worried not about whether they could be happy or fit in, but about what other people's expectations would do to them.

I'd grown up in Orangeburg, in an environment where achievement was expected as the normal order of things. At Felton it never occurred to our stern teachers that we might fail. Now, in Arlington, all we wanted for our sons was that same basic assumption. All we wanted were schools that demanded and expected excellence from our two young "black males"; schools with teachers who, when the boys slipped, didn't just shrug fatalistically at the inevitability of it all and consign them to perpetual victimhood; schools that believed they were fated to succeed rather than fail. It turned out that this was apparently an awful lot to ask for.

We put Aaron into our neighborhood public school in Arlington, and then spent a semester convincing ourselves that everything was going well. The private school he'd attended in London had been especially rigorous, befitting its status as one of the training grounds for the British elite, and so in most subjects he was far ahead of his counterparts in Arlington. He did well, and seemed quite happy. But his teacher, a dedicated and talented woman who also happened to be African American, kept asking one question whenever we had parent-teacher conferences: "What are you going to do with him?"

I didn't understand what she meant—didn't get the sense that anything needed to be done with Aaron—until the following fall, when he went into middle school. As any parent knows, middle school is a minefield. Suddenly he wasn't so comfortable, wasn't so motivated, wasn't so happy.

To the principal, whom we liked, he was a trophy: an African-American boy who made the honor roll, scored off the charts on standardized tests, played trombone in the band. At the annual awards ceremony for the school system he routinely got more certificates and ribbons and medals than anybody else. But it became clear to us that he wasn't enjoying himself. There were lots of problems. The work wasn't challenging enough, some kids were bullies, the classes were so huge he couldn't get a word in edgewise. This wasn't what he was used to, and he didn't particularly like it.

There seemed to be more bothering him, though, and it turned out that there was. He just wasn't on the same wavelength as the other African-American students as far as work and achievement were concerned. He was serious about doing well, and that wasn't cool. Taking the whole thing seriously was nerdish behavior, "white" behavior. The other black students sometimes seemed to take pride in his accomplishments, but more often acted as if they were above that sort of thing.

Once, close to tears, he blurted out to Avis, "They tease me when I do well and they tease me when I don't. What am I supposed to do?"

The teachers were of little help. Generally they treated him well enough, although a few clearly had no real confidence in him and seemed to be just waiting for him to slip. But the teachers had no real sense of his status within the various groups he belonged to: "the boys," "the smart students," "the black students," "the tall students," "the trombone players." These groups didn't necessarily overlap, and they pulled him in conflicting directions. The teachers and the administrators had no answers, and he was pretty miserable.

So we yanked him out and put him in a private school. That was what so many other black parents of academically talented kids had done that there hardly remained a critical mass of achievement-oriented black students in the public school system, not even in enlightened, suburban Arlington. But private school had its own issues, chief among them, for me at least, an enormous sense of isolation from the real world, especially from the real black world.

One of his classmates lived in a single-family house that looked as large as a medium-size apartment building. Another lived in a house that had a regulation-size basketball court in the basement, installed by a doting father because the kids liked playing ball. Some were good kids, some were brats, almost all were white. Eventually the equations seemed to shift back the other way—the college-prep academics weren't discernibly better than at the public high school, the social issues were no less complex, he wasn't that happy, it cost a king's ransom—and we sent him back to the real world.

Lowell presented different issues. Avis, Aaron, and I had all learned more or less fluent Spanish in Argentina, and we all found it an invaluable skill to have in modern-day America. Our bright idea was to put him into a special bilingual Spanish-English program at one of the public elementary schools, so he'd end up learning Spanish like the rest of us. As an added benefit, he'd get a valuable lesson in multiculturalism: Arlington is home to a growing population of Latino immigrants, and so about half of Lowell's classmates would be of Central American or Mexican heritage. But as was becoming usual, we had out-thought ourselves. Lowell just didn't have any particular interest in speaking or reading Spanish; he'd do it when he had to, but wouldn't go out of his way. So he wasn't really getting the benefit we'd hoped for. At the same time, the price we were paying for that unrealized benefit kept climbing: He wasn't getting enough meat-and-potatoes education, since at any given time half the class had only a tenuous idea of what the teacher was saying, they had to proceed more slowly through the material than the teachers at other schools did. The idea was that eventually they would catch up, but Lowell seemed to be missing a lot.

Also, and more strikingly, we seemed to be running into subtle negative assumptions that were being made by the teachers about the Latino kids in Lowell's class and their immigrant parents. The attitude seemed to be: They don't really care about school, their parents don't really care about school, so why should we push them to excel? It disturbed me that this mindset seemed to be at work, and it disturbed me even more that Lowell was getting shortchanged in the process. In the end, Avis and I agreed that he needed more rigor and structure. Our solution was to send him to a local Catholic school.

Back in America we were groping in our attempts to get our boys situated. It's just not easy to raise African-American boys these days, we discovered. I suppose it wasn't easy when my parents raised me, either, but now every step seems so precarious, every precipice so fatal. One slip, it seems, and we could lose them — in a society where black men are not likely to get a second chance.

This was going to be hard work. I was home.

MUCH ABOUT AMERICA looked the same as when I had left, or much the same, but I did see color with new eyes. I'd look around me on the streets of Chocolate City and I'd see not just black people but individuals who were beige, tan, chocolate, ebon, mahogany, "after midnight," high yellow, red, and all the other shades of black. It was really the first time I'd looked at black America the way I'd earlier looked at black Brazil, as anything but monochromatic, as a collection of hues across a range so wide that as color per se they had not all that much to do with one another.

I didn't give color the same meaning or importance that the Brazilians had given it, by any means. But I *saw* it. Without really intending to I had conquered the reflex to ignore the evidence of my eyes, to ignore color as a physical fact. What had been a "black" community was now a brown, beige, tan, and mahogany community, as if the movie had suddenly shifted from black-and-white to Technicolor.

But the social, political, and racial debate seemed drearily unchanged. The black community needed economic development. Affirmative action was controversial. The inner city was bleeding. African Americans had to choose between integration and self-reliance, between seeking to join the mainstream and cultivating self-empowerment. Some black people were better off, some were worse off, and everyone was still talking constantly about race, just like they talked constantly about the weather—with precisely the same ability, it seemed, to do anything about it.

This lack of meaningful change, this sameness, began to get me down. I knew that expatriates often experienced a letdown on returning home, and I told myself this was just a temporary slump, but the truth is that I wondered whether coming back hadn't been a mistake. What I didn't yet fully realize was that regardless of whether America had changed, I certainly had. What I had learned and understood about race while I was abroad gave me a new way to confront the issues of race at home.

My new title was foreign editor, and in addition to my management duties, I felt that if I were going to do my job well, I also had an obligation to participate in the broader debate about foreign affairs. In due course I began receiving, and accepting, invitations to give talks and participate in seminars. One day, a few months after our return, I was asked to sit on a panel on press coverage of Africa that was being held at Howard University.

Howard was one of the citadels of African-American scholarship, and it was a place that had always intimidated me. I was familiar enough with the place: Howard was one of the major institutions of black Washington, and so as a reporter and editor on the local staff I'd had many an occasion over the years to go up to the hilltop campus for stories or events. I never had any real regrets about my decision not to attend Howard, Morehouse, or any other of the historically black colleges—not even after my sister Ellen had gone to Spelman and become so committed to that path. But sometimes I did wonder what my life would have been like if I'd made the other choice. Stepping onto the Howard campus always launched that line of thought, and also made me feel a bit defensive. I always felt, for some reason, that my decision not to go to a black school was called into question and I was obliged to defend it.

Black colleges were keepers of traditions that so many others, including my own family, participated in, yet about which I knew next to nothing. I didn't belong to a black fraternity, for example. I could have joined any of the major ones at Michigan, like Alpha Phi Alpha or Omega Psi Phi, but I wasn't a joiner and anyway there was very little pressure on such a large campus to conform. But on a smaller, all-black campus, would the pressure have been more intense? Or would I have just seen things differently and wanted to join? My mother and my sister are Deltas; my father, an Alpha. All my adult life I'd seen black men meet for the first time and discover they were both Alphas or both Omegas, and from that one fact forge an instant bond, begin a conversation from which I was excluded. That was what going to Howard always had felt like, going to a place where you're left out of an important part of the conversation.

But I was glad to participate in the panel—I felt strongly that this kind of public appearance was part of my job. So I drove over to the campus, spent fifteen minutes looking for a parking space, found my name card on the dais in a meeting room at Crampton Auditorium, and sat there for a couple of hours taking my lumps.

It was a familiar scene: There I was, the representative of a powerful white media empire, being grilled by a black audience that felt mistreated. In this case many in the audience were either African-born academics or American-born students or activists interested in the African continent. They were loaded for bear. Why didn't the *Post* have more coverage of Africa? Why did the *Post's* coverage of the continent consist solely of war and disaster? Why was the carnage in Sierra Leone being ignored? Why weren't more stories about Africa appearing on the front page?

With each question I felt a bit more deflated. It could have been a decade earlier, and I could have been out covering Marion Barry or school board forums, and the questions could have been about why the *Post* was trying to destroy black Washington.

I started in by giving my standard answers, my semidefensive patter—and then I stopped.

I realized something about the questions, and about the questioners, that I hadn't understood before. They were looking for answers not just from an editor at the *Post*, but from a *black* editor at the *Post*. That sounds absurdly trivial, but it's not. My position was only part of what I brought before the audience. I also brought my experience as an African-American professional, my roots in the South, my status as a black husband and as the black father of two black sons. It was all relevant here.

That was when I realized that I had changed, that I was a different person now, and that I had really come home.

I began to answer from the heart. Now the truth is that the substance of my answers didn't really change at all. I really thought we were doing a creditable job covering Africa—not perfect, of course, but as good a job as anyone else. But I dropped the defensiveness and took off the armor. I engaged with the questions and the questioners, rather than fending them off. If they were wrong, I told them so; and when I argued with my interrogators, it felt less like a formal disagreement than a family row.

Afterward, I lingered to chat with a few of the audience members, including a group of students. I stood there for a long time, talking about Liberia and South Africa and Nigeria, trying to give honest answers even if they weren't the answers the students wanted to hear, and I felt something that I hadn't let myself feel all those years ago when I had been out in black Washington representing the white *Washington Post*. Or maybe I just hadn't been ready to feel it. It was pride that I felt, the pride that they seemed to feel in me, despite never having met me before and not really knowing anything about me—anything, that is, except my race. That day at Howard I was a part of the conversation, the entire conversation.

A lot of things had changed. I was older, I had a more senior position, I was just generally more experienced and more confident. But I also had the benefit of the time I'd spent overseas and the lessons I'd learned about race, about identity, about anger, about color, about group, about myself. It wasn't about separation or exclusivity or anything like that. It had nothing to do with rejecting any part of my life or my history; I was comfortable with the decisions that I had made, including the decision to live and work in the white world, to have white friends and consider myself a participant in American culture in the widest possible sense. But I was also comfortable, more comfortable than I'd ever been, with the conviction that none of these decisions were in conflict with the important role that race had to play in my private and public life. I was comfortable with race as a base, a framework, a starting point. I was eager to be embraced by it, to draw support and power from it, to use it to connect me to a wider community through shared history, shared culture, shared dreams. I felt—I *knew*—that race was not obsolete, at least for this middle-aged African-American man, that it was still important for me to give and receive race's pride.

So at Howard I had talked from the heart. I'd found a way to live in America.

Chapter 13

Home

THIS IS ABOUT REALLY GOING HOME.

Not home to America, home to the South. That's one important distinction; here's another: This is about going home to the
New South, as opposed to the Old South that I had left behind all
those years ago, with barely a backward glance. I'd been back
dozens of times for quick visits, of course, but not to examine, not
to assess.

It's all different now, and all the same, and still all about race,
all about color.

THE HEADLINES WERE shocking, and all the more shocking because they were in such small type, at least in my newspaper, and
so hard to find back there in the nether regions of the first news

section: another black church had burned to the ground in the South, and another, and still another. It went on and on until it made me angry, and then alarmed, and then genuinely frightened. What made me almost as mad as the church burnings themselves was the fact that the *Post,* one of the handful of newspapers with the power to single-handedly put an issue onto the national agenda, seemed to be awfully slow to recognize that this was a real story, a major story. Granted, it's hard to see the overall significance of something that happens in increments, but at some point, after running a dozen little short items inside where hardly anyone would see them, the time comes to step back and do a major piece aimed for the front page. I believed we'd been slow to bring the story out front where it belonged, and in one of our Monday morning editors' meetings I said so.

We ended up having a long, meandering discussion about the South. Then somehow, it became more of a monologue about my experiences growing up in Orangeburg, my parents' take on the church burnings, my suspicions and fears of Klan activity, my feeling that we needed to do something major on the issue of race. This was the summer of 1996, and the Olympics were due to start in Atlanta in a couple of months; between the games and the arson attacks, I argued, we had ample excuse to tale a full-bore look at race relations in the South.

Great idea, said my colleagues on the national desk, and since you seem to have so many bright ideas about it, you're going to help out.

We sketched out a planned series of articles. My assignment was to go to some small town in the South and write about the texture of relations between blacks and whites. I decided it would be interesting to go to a state I'd never visited, so I picked Alabama. Deb Heard, an editor in the Style section, is an African

American who grew up in a small town in Alabama, so I asked her where I should go. She put me in touch with her mother, who was full of sound advice, and after a round of consultations I settled on Lineville, Alabama, population, 2,394.

Tucked into the hilly uplands of northern Alabama, Lineville is hardly more than a crossroads. Downtown consists of a stretch of old brick buildings—they would be charming if restored— joined together by a kind of covered sidewalk that was somebody's idea of urban renewal. It's about 60 percent white and 40 percent black, and like most little towns in the South it used to be a farming community. But hardly anyone can make a decent living on a family farm anymore. Most people work in the textile plants, or for manufacturers like Wellborn Cabinet, or in the big Tyson Foods poultry plant five miles away in Ashland, the county seat. Years ago, farmers in overalls and work boots used to clump through town; today, wage-earning women run midday errands in their Japanese cars, wearing the puffy plastic hair nets that Tyson requires on the line.

I didn't have any appointments set up in advance, so I headed for Lineville's tiny city hall, a modern little building that looks like a public library branch, and asked to see the mayor. An aide asked me to have a seat, and then went into the back, presumably to phone His Honor and let him know a reporter was waiting to see him. About fifteen minutes later, in walked Mayor Perry Young, a man I had to try with all my might not to dislike at first glance.

Mayor Young ushered me into his office, which was littered with street signs and stop signs—replacements for signs stolen by vandals, shot up by target-shooters, or flattened by veering drunks—and offered me a seat. He was tall, white-haired, of course white, and looked to be in his sixties. The minute he opened his mouth and I heard his accent I felt myself becoming tense and aggressive, perhaps unprofessionally so. That particular combination of attributes—an older white man with white hair and a southern accent in a position of authority—brought to mind the mayors and police chiefs and school superintendents of my youth in Orangeburg, drawling old white-haired white men all. These were people I had detested. I had no good reason to detest Perry Young, but I had no good reason to like him either.

I guess I must have been expecting a fight, because I was surprised to find him gracious, respectful, and open, although only to a point.

There had been no church burnings in Lineville, but everyone was aware of them, and naturally everyone wondered whether this little community might be next. I asked about the general state of relations between black and white in his town; the mayor, as I'd expected, said that as far as he could tell, things were just fine.

"You hear prejudice on both sides," he said, "but I believe deep down in everybody's hearts, we know we're all here for the same purpose." It was a kind of canned, oversimplified, Bible Belt view of an enormously complex set of interactions. Yet he did seem to be engaging the question and trying to deal with it head-on. He did seem to be thinking. That's just the way he thought.

"Blacks and whites go to school together, and there's some that go to church together," he said. "And they're intermarrying. Not so much intermarrying, but dating, or going together. At least, that is what I hear. I don't see it much myself. I hear about it as much from the blacks as from the whites."

Then he drifted into talking about the old days. I imagined, cynically—yes, cynically, but I felt entitled—that he would

soon express his wistful longing for the days when nigras knew
their place and all that, but of course he did no such thing. Even
Lineville observes strictures of political correctness. Rather, he
wanted to talk about the halcyon days in an economic sense,
rather than social or racial. For most of his adult life, he was a
storekeeper. He had a dry-goods store, he said, and it was a
pretty good living. But then Wal-Mart moved into the area
about ten years ago, opening five stores within a thirty-five-mile
radius of Lineville: "They took my bread-and-butter items and
they sold 'em for what I had to pay to get 'em. I held on for three
or four more years, but it was no use." So he bailed out. It was a
rational decision, but I could tell how much it must have hurt to
make it.

I brought us back to race. Mayor Young considered it, essentially, yesterday's news. There had been terrible prejudice against
blacks, he said, and whites had been the offenders. But now
things had changed, and white people's attitudes had changed,
and so, basically, end of story. He seemed particularly perplexed
that blacks kept throwing the past in his face and in the faces of
the other white people of Lineville: "The way I feel, there
shouldn't be any prejudice towards whites because of all of that
happened before. That ought to be left behind us."

Then the mayor got to the subject he really wanted to talk
about, and I realized that, like any politician, he intended to use
the visiting press to send a message. His preoccupation was "the
Mexicans," the several hundred immigrants from Mexico, Cuba,
and Central America who had recently settled in Lineville and
surrounding Clay County. Many worked at the Tyson plant; they
tended to live in house trailers, seven or eight to a little trailer that
could barely hold a family of four; they were showing up in the
schools, which weren't prepared to handle them; they were

showing up in the courts, and there was no money to pay for interpreters; they were terrible drivers:

"We don't have room for them and we don't have money for them. They're good people, but we feel like they're going to have to adapt to us, not us adapt to them."

When he talked about the Latinos he assumed a kind of intimacy with me that he hadn't assumed before. He seemed to be saying: We know each other, you and me. We've been bound together for three hundred years, and whether or not we like each other, we understand each other. We couldn't escape each other if we wanted to. But these other people, they're different. We might not be able to agree on much, but we can agree on that: They're different, and we have to protect our interests against theirs.

I left the mayor's office stunned. That was the first and last time that a white southerner had ever tried to enlist me as an ally in the camp that had the money and the power and the comfortable situation, and that looked down on the "other" camp, which was poor and powerless and miserable but still determined to rise in the world, perhaps at "our" camp's expense. An old white-haired southerner standing arm-in-arm with his black neighbors against the advancing Latin hordes? Did this mean that things had really changed?

No, it didn't. Things hadn't changed that much at all.

I'd asked Mayor Young if there were any black clergymen I might talk to, people who would obviously be concerned about the possibility of church burnings, and he sent me to see the Reverend Charles Caldwell. To get to his house I drove to the other side of town, across the railroad tracks, and then down into a little bottomland neighborhood of narrow streets and tiny houses and vacant lots overgrown with kudzu. This was one of the two main black neighborhoods in the town. You could tell a lot about the unemployment rate among blacks in Lineville by the number of young men, at midday, washing or working on their cars, and by the number of houses where you heard soap operas blaring from television sets as you rolled past. I'd go a ways, ask somebody where Reverend Caldwell lived, and get such an indeterminate response—a nod or a wave in the direction I was already heading, no more—that I'd have to stop again in the next block. Finally, I got to a house where a dark-skinned man in his fifties answered simply, "I'm Reverend Caldwell."

The minister was sitting on his little front porch, passing the day; he had to go to his church, Macedonia Baptist, for a prayer meeting later that evening, but that was hours away. A young man from the neighborhood, Tommy Lee, was sitting with him. They were idle in a way that only people in the South know how to be idle, content in their stillness, floating in the currents of the afternoon like a leaf in a lazy stream. Someone would walk past—they would speak. Someone else would walk past—they would nod, or wave. They weren't waiting to do anything, weren't late to go anywhere, weren't torn in a million directions like most of us are when we try to sit still. They just were. This is something I remember well from my own childhood, when we'd all sit on the front porch in Orangeburg and watch evening flow into night. Porch-sitting in the South is the closest thing our society has to Zen.

So I came up onto Reverend Caldwell's porch and sat with him and Tommy Lee. I sat the way you're supposed to sit, mostly in silence. It must have taken me a half-hour to impart to him the basic information that I was an editor for the *Washington Post*, that I was in Lineville doing a story about race, and that I wanted to hear what he thought about the church burnings specifically and about race relations in general in his small Alabama town.

I knew he was a preacher, and I thought he might answer in the form of a sermon. But he didn't wind up. He just very quietly told a story about growing up on a farm a few miles away from Lineville and remembering "as clear as yesterday" the night the Klan came, the night they dug a shallow trench in the form of a cross in front of his family's farmhouse and filled it with gasoline and set it ablaze.

Things were better now, he guessed.

His wife, Ora, came home for lunch from her factory job; she brought Reverend Caldwell a plate of food, and the two of them ate there on the porch while they talked with me. She was the one who seemed to want to preach. She said things hadn't really changed that much at all. Blacks could get jobs, but no matter how well they did, whites got the promotions and ended up being the supervisors, getting the extra pay. Right over in the next county, the principal of the high school had made the national news when he threatened to cancel the prom because he objected to interracial dating. And where was this principal now? He was about to be elected superintendent of schools, that's where.

"People make me sick," Ora Caldwell said. "In a way things are better, and in a way not." She would have liked to tell me more, she said, but she had to get back to work; she'd get docked if she were late.

From there I went to the part of town called Kudzu Hill to meet a certified black success story. In a modest but immaculately kept mobile home, in what had once been the most crime-ridden and drug-infested part of town, lived Norman Gibbons, city councilman. Gibbons was one of two black council members elected after the U.S. Justice Department compelled the city to switch to district-based voting, instead of filling all the seats at-large, so that black candidates would have a chance.

Gibbons had been a star athlete at the local integrated high school, lettering in both football and basketball. Later he went to Tuskegee Institute and Jacksonville State University, graduating with a degree in business; he had been snapped up by the Hardee's fast-food chain upon graduation, apprenticed all over the South, and now managed the Hardee's five miles away in Ashland, doing a million dollars' worth of business a year.

We sat in his small living room, and it quickly became clear that he intended to speak carefully. Race was a sensitive topic, and he was a public official. Whites he went to high school with were still among his closest friends, he said: "I really feel that if you work hard, if you're willing to go out and get your own, you can be anything you want to be. Any race has both the good and the bad. Some of my best friends are white. Prejudice is not inherited through your genes. I feel it's taught, in all races."

Fair enough, and perhaps to be expected from a small-town Babbitt—a Babbitt with all the good, solid, middle-class values that implies. But then he relaxed a bit, and kept talking. He told me how he had gotten into politics.

His brother Charles had been an even better athlete, even more of a local star. The sky was the limit for Charles—he was bright, charismatic, alive with possibility. Then one day he was pulled over by a certain Lineville policeman, a thug hired from out of town "to come down and straighten out the black folks." It should have been routine traffic stop, but before it was over, the officer had beaten Charles Gibbons so severely with a flashlight that he almost died. He now has a metal plate in his head, experiences flashbacks, and collects disability, his dreams permanently deferred.

"I got into politics so nothing like that would ever happen again, " Norman Gibbons said.

The officer who beat Charles Gibbons is long gone, and so are the mayor and police chief who hired him. I went to the police station to meet the current chief, Larry Whatley, and was nothing less than stunned at how enlightened he seemed. Everything and everyone else in Lineville had basically conformed to my idea of what the small-town South was like, but here was a man who didn't seem hypocritical, didn't seem to want to sweep race under the rug, didn't seem to want to make color the governing fact of his life either. Talking about the Hispanics, he said: "There's really more tension about that than any race problem. Ignorance breeds hate, and stereotypes breed ignorance. The only real problem we have with the Hispanics is their driving ability."

I thought that was a remarkable thing for a white southern sheriff to say. Maybe some things — or at least some people — had changed more than I thought.

I WENT BACK to Washington and wrote my story. It turned out fine, I thought: It was evenhanded, gave both whites and blacks their say, explained that racism still existed but also that things had significantly changed, introduced some vivid characters, and pretty well captured the pace and the feel of the little town I'd chosen. But in the end, like almost all newspaper stories, it left the really important things unsaid. The newspaper form generally doesn't allow the writer to express his feelings and emotions, and in this case feelings and emotions were by far the most important part of the experience.

I'd never met any of the people of Lineville before in my life, and yet I felt I knew all of them quite well — all except the police chief, that is, who was something new. The rest were so familiar as to seem archetypal. There were the newly sensitive white folks determined to show me how much they had changed, the newly ambitious black folks careful of what they said, the salt-of-the-earth preacher and his saltier wife. There was even a diner with heart-of-gold waitresses, and there were any number of gas stations with Goober Pyle sticking his head out from under somebody's car to speak on behalf of the working man.

There were third-worldish extremes: a little all-white neighborhood up near the high school, with big comfortable houses nestled amid the tall pines, and on the other side of town Kudzu Hill, with its trailers and its raw hillsides and its sullen young men idling the day away.

There were colors, stark contrasting colors, white people almost pinkish despite the hot sun, black people darker than rosewood.

And it was all just a bit maddening to me. It's often pointed out—especially, in my experience, by white southerners—that black people and white people have a more intimate and familiar coexistence in the South than in other parts of the country. This fact is often proffered as evidence that race relations are actually better in the New South than elsewhere in America, since in many ways there's less overt friction. White southerners say to black southerners, essentially, "We've changed, we're sorry, but now we're on equal footing, so let's get on with our lives. We know each other too well to fight. Let's all just let bygones be bygones." But of course that completely ignores the fact that there is no equal footing. The basic relationships of power and wealth haven't changed fundamentally, haven't even begun to change, really, except possibly in Atlanta and maybe one or two other big cities. The reasons why the black neighborhoods of Lineville consist mainly of cramped little houses or mobile homes, while the well-to-do areas are all white, have to do with those soon-to-be-forgotten "bygones." Basic inequalities have been frozen in place, and instead of dealing with them through demands and conflict and negotiation, everybody is just supposed to hug and move on.

This is the New South, and as nice and hospitable as the people of Lineville were, I wished that some of them would just open their damned eyes and that others would just go straight to Hell.

LINEVILLE WAS JUST prelude, however. For me, going home meant going back to Orangeburg and trying to see it with new eyes.

I say "trying" because it's hard to see a landscape that you know as intimately as the back of your hand. When everything seems so obvious, so self-evident, then nothing seems remarkable. Familiarity flattens hills, lifts valleys, narrows rivers into streams and lakes into ponds; it diminishes and dims.

Home, it turns out, isn't what it used to be. And, of course, neither am I.

The one thing that hasn't changed, to speak of, is our house. My parents still live there, occupying the big, high-ceilinged rooms where my mother grew up and where her mother grew up. The only real difference from the outside is that it's now partially hidden from the street by a big magnolia tree. I remember when my father planted it, a scrawny little thing that I could easily hurdle. Now it towers over the house, littering the front yard with the leaves it constantly sheds. That house is like an anchor in my life, an absolute point of reference, a fixed center. There is no place on Earth where I feel quite the same.

That house, built by Major John Hammond Fordham nearly a century ago, is now registered on a list of historic places. A portrait of the house, minus the obscuring magnolia, hangs in the Prince of Orange Mall, the "new" mall, out on the road that leads to the nearby town of North, South Carolina. While I was in high school, the "old" mall—about a mile closer to town—pretty much finished off the old downtown. It was a decade later when the new mall killed off the old mall. Now, in the brutal Darwinism of small-town America, a Wal-Mart has pretty much killed off the new mall as well.

Wal-Mart is not far from the old Wade Hampton Academy, founded after the schools were integrated as a final refuge for whites who wouldn't abide having their children sit in classrooms next to boys and girls whose skin was brown. Back when I was going to Orangeburg High, every year a few of my white classmates would defect to Wade Hampton and blessed refuge in an all-white sanctuary. Today, astoundingly, what distinguishes Wade Hampton is its Christian orientation, not its racial policies. There are black students attending Wade Hampton, which in my universe is supposed to happen the day after Hell freezes solid.

Driving around town I see that the place has grown to the point where it is almost possible—almost, but not quite—for me to get lost. Neighborhoods that used to tail off into farmland now continue; fields and even swamps have become little shopping areas; whole subdivisions are hiding out there amid the deep pines. There is traffic, and a modicum of bustle. But there still isn't anything really metropolitan about Orangeburg. It is a much bigger small town than the one I remembered, but a small town still.

Not everything has grown. Claflin College, where my mother had been the head librarian, seems to have stalled. This is the story for so many historically black colleges around the South, especially the private or church-sponsored schools like Claflin (which is affiliated with the Methodist Church). Put simply, black students have far more options these days. Students who once might have gone to Claflin, and been happy to do so, can now go to the University of South Carolina, or Clemson, or even the Citadel. Claflin is no match for these schools. Its old brick buildings are as stately as ever, but the forlorn look of the campus—and the dull-eyed look of the students—signals that the school has come down in the world.

Right next door, however, South Carolina State College is thriving, its name and status having been upgraded to South Carolina State University. The state government, vulnerable to the votes of black state legislators and the written orders of federal judges, has vastly increased funding for this state-supported institution of higher learning over the years. The campus has grown dramatically, there are a host of new buildings, and the old ones I remembered from my youth have been well-maintained. The old four-room Felton Training School is long gone, replaced by a soulless modern structure; gone, too, is White Auditorium, where Felton used to stage an annual operetta (I played Rumplestiltskin, in blue tights). There is a new business school, where my sister Ellen teaches marketing. Her students look sharp and bright, but when they call her "Ms. Robinson" I cannot resist an older brother's smirk. She has her own house now, her own life, and she makes me awfully proud.

My aunt Georgia is thinking about buying a new house, and so Ellen takes me to see it. We drive way out along the river to a place where there used to be nothing but Spanish moss and water moccasins, until Ellen pulls into a new subdivision called Eddisto Plantation. We see large, custom-built houses arrayed around a man-made lake—beautiful and spacious but not especially remarkable, until I consider the context. This is an integrated sub-division, with white families, black families, and even an Asian family I see working in their front yard. Such a thing simply couldn't have existed in the Orangeburg I remembered. And the thought of African Americans, in Orangeburg of all places, vol-untarily living in a place that calls itself a "plantation" is just too much for me.

All this is incredible. But there are other changes that are not so welcome.

The town now faces a new kind of menace, a new kind of vi-olence in the air. Orangeburg is just a few miles off Interstate 95, the cocaine pipeline from Miami to Washington, New York, and all the other cities of the east coast. Crack has come to Orange-burg, and with it the rank desperation and ruined lives of addic-tion, along with the purposeful mayhem of serious drug dealing. I find that the drug's arrival is something everyone wanted to talk about, but even before being told I could sense it, I could see it in the sullen looks I got from people, or the glassy stares, or the furtive glances. People have alarm systems in their houses now; single women often carry guns. Customized low-riders and shiny new four-by-fours idle at stoplights, tape players turned up so loud that the thumping bass lines of foul-mouthed, posthumous hits by Notorious B.I.G. or Tupac Shakur shake the fillings in my teeth, three car-lengths away.

On a walk to the neighborhood community center a long block away at the end of Oak Street, Avis and I see a group of six or seven older boys discussing something, then arguing, and then for no apparent reason one of them jumps another, bashes him to the ground and keeps hitting him, as hard as he could, while the others just stand by. The whole incident lasts just a few minutes. Nobody is seriously injured, but we are shaken by the casual nature of the violence, arising and then blowing over as suddenly as a summer squall.

With the benefit of my new eyes I now see color for the first time in Orangeburg, and through color I see race.

If Orangeburg were a town in Brazil I would be astounded at the extent to which black people and white people live sepa- rately—in separate neighborhoods, going to separate churches, leading separate lives. Not even in Planaltina, the little town out- side Brasília where I'd first noticed a system that looked almost like apartheid, was the separation so complete. I'd be surprised at not seeing interracial couples walking hand-in-hand down the street. I would expect to see a lot more children of obviously mixed heritage.

I drive through Sunnyside, the old neighborhood of shacks and alleys, and I see that little has changed. The people still look the same; they move slowly in the noonday heat, as if there is no energy inside them, as if all the vital force has somehow been drained away. If this were Brazil I would notice that these people are very dark-skinned, and I would make the connection. I would compare the people in Sunnyside to the students and pro- fessors at Claflin and S. C. State, with their range of skin tones, and I would conclude that the blackest people in this society are the most discriminated against, that the darker you are in Amer- ica, or at least in Orangeburg, the greater the odds that you are also ill-fed, ill-housed, ill-clothed, ill-educated, ill-prepared to make your way in the world.

But I also see that that would have been an incomplete pic- ture—incomplete and wrong. I see that whatever role color may play in America, it still plays that role within a larger context of race. I see, in Orangeburg and the rest of America, a context for dealing with inequalities that couldn't possibly exist if all there

were to talk about were a skin-color continuum, a scale of economic and political power in which light made right. We have
more than that. We have a sense, from coal to cream, that we belong to something larger, something more powerful, something
more purposeful, something that's not about shutting doors,
that's not about excluding whites or Latinos or Asians or anybody else, but about establishing a framework from which to
reach out, both as individuals and as a group. We have great di-
versity, but also the potential for great unity.

We have one another, and in that we have strength.

COMING OUT OF the S. C. State campus one day my eye falls on a
familiar white house with big Tara-like columns, and I notice a
stream of black women going in and out. It is Mike O'Cain's
house, the house where I listened to Bob Dylan with my one
white Orangeburg friend. This emblem of the Old South has
since been sold and is now being used by a black sorority.

As for Mike himself, he went on to college and then veteri-
nary school. For many years he took care of my parents' dogs, including Buffalo, the Norwegian elkhound I'd acquired in college
and then left with them "temporarily," which meant until the end
of his long life. A couple of times while I was in town my father
asked me to help him take the dogs in for some shot or treatment;
I'd see Mike and we'd chat for a while, but there was never really
time to talk.

Then one year we took the dogs to another vet. It turned out
that Mike had sold his business and left the profession. My folks
were unclear on just what he was doing or why. But they had a
phone number. The next time I was in town, I called it. Mike answered and invited me out to see his dream.

I followed his directions and found myself about five miles outside of town, at the end of a driveway through the woods, knocking at the door of a cabin next to a little lake.

Mike had ditched his career as a veterinarian, selling everything and ridding himself of all encumbrances, to acquire this cabin and this piece of land, where he intended to grow camellias. These gaudy southern flowers were much prized, and people would pay a fortune for them. He figured there was a living to be made in camellias if he worked hard enough at it and could summon enough patience.

Across the lake, his dream was taking shape: He had spent months clearing land for his plantings. Despite his markedly weakened legs Mike had spent months, working alone with a little tractor and a chain saw, cutting down trees and rooting out stumps and hauling everything away. I was both astonished and perplexed, but at the same time I was glad to see he was so obviously happy.

We toured the field and then went back to the cabin, where we sat on the porch and drank beer and told each other our recent life stories. He was single; he had been unlucky in love, and at the moment was feeling especially betrayed, his most recent breakup having happened only recently. He spoke with some bitterness about his father, who had always wanted him to be someone else. While we talked several dogs milled about—big dogs, the kind it would take somebody like a vet to handle, animals with a lot of nobility and wildness left in them. These looked like guard dogs.

He asked what it had been like to travel around the world, and I told him. I asked what it had been like to stay in Orangeburg, and he told me.

This was now a bad, bad place, he said. People were getting robbed at knifepoint, at gunpoint, and they'd just as soon kill you as not. There was a lot of anger. The town was full of crazy folks, crazy black folks and crazy white folks. There could be an explosion, and it could happen any day. But he felt safe out here, he said, in his cabin, next to his lake. Probably nothing bad would happen. But if it did, he was ready. They'd have to come in after him, and he was ready.

We drank our beer and chatted for a while. As I was leaving an acquaintance of Mike's came by to bring him a rifle that he'd either lent out or sent for repairs. Here I was, alone with a couple of southern white men, a pack of dogs, and a rifle in the deep woods, and I was fairly sure I'd leave with my life. Orangeburg had come a long way, for better or worse. Mike and I had come a long way since Bob Dylan, both of us, but we could still talk easily and enjoy each other's company.

We'd both changed, I suppose. I certainly had.

I realized that all those years ago, sitting in Mike's room and listening to Dylan, I'd been trying to broaden myself, to reach out to the wider world, to expand—but also to shed something. To become just a person, not a black person. Over the next two decades I'd pursued this goal, without any real intent and certainly without any real direction, until finally I went overseas and made my first trip to Brazil and became convinced that I'd attained the raceless state I was seeking. I felt I could fly, felt I could soar.

But then I saw what it meant when black people, looking up from the bottom of a society, lived without a sense of racial identity. I came to appreciate the measure of power and pride they were denying themselves. I realized how much language mattered, how much vocabulary mattered, how much race mattered. I came to see blackness—blackness as identity, which I once considered an outdated and irrelevant concept—as something deeply important to me and every other black person in America, and as vitally current. It wasn't yesterday's news; it was tomorrow's.

I went back to the house and looked up at those old portraits of my great-grandfather and great-grandmother, those portraits of coal and cream, and I saw a spectrum, a range, a continuum. An identity. An impulse. A shield. A refuge. A home.

One in a Million

BACK HOME IN AMERICA, SETTLED INTO AN APPROXIMATION OF my former life, I sat in my office that October morning, fidgety, distracted, until I couldn't take it any more, and then I slipped out to take a purposeful walk.

The streets of Washington were unnaturally quiet for a weekday: The federal government had given the bureaucracy permission not to come in, and naked fear had kept many other downtown workers home in the suburbs. This was supposed to be a day of chaos, according to the conventional wisdom. At best, the television anchorpeople had warned, there would be monumental gridlock from dawn 'til dusk. At worst—and this was just implied, never flat-out said—there could be violence, even anarchy, an explosion of incalculable force and disastrous consequences. Many men were approaching the nation's capital. The beige, tan, brown, and browner skin these men had the poor fashion sense to wear marked them as the angriest people in America, certainly the most dangerous. The approach of only three or four of them was enough to send many people scurrying to the other side of the street. Today there would be no opposite sidewalk to run to—inappropriately colored men would be over there, too.

From the distance came a dim roar, faint but with such power that I didn't hear it so much as feel it. Grabbing my jacket and heading out to the street, I walked south toward the White House and the Mall. A glance around: All the pedestrians I could see were black men, all of us going vaguely in the same direction. This was a strange sensation at first, at least for me, almost a guilty sensation, as if we were doing something we weren't supposed to. We weren't blind: We could see as well as anyone else that our colors were the unloved colors, the undeserving ones.

I was suddenly self-conscious, not of my skin color but of my coat and tie, which immediately marked me as having come from the office. From the way they were dressed it was obvious that most of the men around me had heeded the call to take the day off from work as a gesture of commitment and atonement. Wasn't I showing my own commitment to be less than complete? I expected looks of reproach; from many years of wearing this impolitic skin I was accustomed to being eyed with reproach. But none in the swelling crowd seemed to want to judge me, and in this sudden absence of judgment I stood taller, stepped livelier.

In small groups or by themselves men swung out of side streets to join our main stream heading south toward the Mall. There were hip-hoppers in Tommy Hilfiger jackets and knit caps; gray-bearded businessmen in Italian suits and Gucci loafers; lunch-bucket guys-next-door with advancing bellies and receding hairlines. There was a tall, skinny, light-skinned man in overalls and dreadlocks walking next to a short, pudgy, much darker guy in warm-ups with his little son on his shoulders. There were big families, grandfathers and uncles and dads and sons and nephews and cousins, often in wildly different shades of brown but with the same telltale hooked nose or huge ears. Big brothers led little brothers by the hand. A white-on-white Lincoln Continental slipped into a parking space, and out stepped two gold-chain-dripping, black-silk-shirted, diamond-pinkie-ringed refugees from a Superfly movie, who fell in with our ragged file.

This was interesting.

Just past McPherson Square we met the first couple of vendors. One was selling bottles of spring water; the other, T-shirts and bumper stickers that said, I ATTENDED THE MILLION MAN MARCH.

Part of Pennsylvania Avenue had been closed to cars earlier in the year because of the potential threat of terrorist attack, and as we passed by I noticed there was a heavier-than-usual police presence guarding the approach to the White House. But there was no electricity as we passed the cops, no crackle of fire arcing between opposite charges, not even when the youngbloods went by in their superbaggy jeans and their knit caps. A transformation was taking place: Our unfortunate colors were becoming the acceptable, even appropriate ones. If only for a day.

As we got closer to the Mall our ranks thickened until we were not a river but a flood, first filling the wide sidewalks and then spilling into the streets. The general flow shifted eastward, but I wanted a sense of perspective so I kept heading due south until I crossed Constitution Avenue and began to climb the hill to the Washington Monument. Already, the sloping greensward was strewn with a blanket of people, beige and brown and browner people, all in motion, all except a few individuals standing stock-still like fixtures; these were the marshals from the Fruit of Islam, dressed in dark suits and white shirts and skinny bow ties.

A family, three generations of cocoa-colored men, posed for a picture with the Monument and the crowd in the background. "This is for history," one of them said.

A dozen men came past, all different hues, stepping like a fraternity pledge line and chanting that they were from Pittsburgh. They drew cheers from the crowd. Another line, this one from Atlanta, came from the other direction and drew even louder cheers.

An old man, very dark, struggled past; someone took him by the arm and helped him along until he found a place to sit and rest.

A group of teenagers, all coal-dark, went past, and I noticed their eyes. I guess I must have been expecting the hard, shuttered gaze that young men so often wear on city streets, because I was surprised at how bright their eyes were, how alive. They saw.

A copper-brown man walked past with his two sons, holding each by the hand. I wished I'd brought my own two boys, and I was ashamed that I'd left them home because of some vague worry about what might happen. It's reasonable to assume that huge crowds will always be somewhat volatile, but I could tell that this one wasn't—that everything would be all right.

Finally I made it all the way up the hill and reached the Monument's base, a height from which I could see all the way down the Mall. The mass of people stretched almost unbroken to the Capitol. I knew immediately that there'd be a big fight over the numbers, but that in the end arithmetic would be irrelevant. All the fervent rage that gathered around Louis Farrakhan, the lightning rod who had brought us together, was also in the end irrelevant. The crowd was more than enough: We were enough.

I wandered down toward the Capitol and just mingled for a while. Of the many sights, sounds, and impressions I took away, there was one I knew I could never forget: Hundreds of thousands of black men were crossing one another's paths, bumping into one another, stepping on one another's toes, and I saw not so much as one angry shove, heard not so much as one muttered imprecation. No alpha-male staredown. Making eye contact was no longer a sign of disrespect serious enough to be a matter of life and death. Suddenly, looking one another in the eye was a gesture of recognition, even of communion. It was like the end of a long, bitter estrangement, a brief glimpse of a possible second chance.

Another impression took longer to form but is even more indelible. We were hundreds of thousands defined as a group by our common color, but that color was common only in the loosest sense: some of us were in fact ebony, others every conceivable shade of brown or red or even yellow, a range that went all the way from coal to cream.

Instead of accepting the wisdom of our society that these were the wrong colors, we flaunted them, our beiges and tans and burnt siennas and browns, and we flaunted them together in an impossibly large group whose size and confidence, a reflection of each individual in turn gave each individual strength. That day, we had come together on our own terms—defining those terms as a range of skin color.

Which, of course, is supposed to be wrong.

The America I came home to was supposed to be moving, finally, toward a nonracial society—a colorblind society. At least that's what I read. Racial walls, finally, were seen to be breaking down. Black people were continuing their movement, physically and psychologically, out of the ghetto into the larger society, to take our rightful places as buttoned-down corporate executives, slick politicians, debt-ridden homeowners, suburban soccer moms, pudgy joggers, weekend golfers, uptight coronary victims, smug and self-satisfied burghers, dyed-in-the-wool Republicans. We'd entered the mainstream. Millions had been left behind, but that was more of an economic issue than a racial one, wasn't it? After all, it was African Americans who were fleeing the inner cities now, even more frantically and definitively than whites did thirty years ago. There were black suburbs of Washington and Atlanta and other cities that were not just middle-class, but out-and-out wealthy. And there was another new development to ponder: Of new marriages involving African Americans, one out of eight was interracial. Wasn't this the ultimate solution to the race question, the advent of thousands of café-au-lait-skinned, curly-haired, hazel-eyed offspring to blur the distinctions between the races into a smooth continuum?

Race was supposed to be yesterday's news. A gathering of a million men based solely on their race ought to be as relevant, in terms of where we go from here, as last Friday's stock quotes. At least that's what I read.

But that's not what I felt that day on the Mall.

I'd spent most of the previous decade in places where race was blurred, or conquered, or obliterated, or simply ignored. I'd seen that you can indeed get rid of race, you can effectively wipe it out, you can end up with a society in which people simply don't think in racial terms, or at least not in what we consider racial terms. But getting rid of racial identity was no panacea. In Brazil, I'd seen a stubborn residue: color. I'd seen that color was capable of producing all the same horrors that race was capable of producing, but worse. It left those at the bottom of the ladder without an identity to hold them together and push them forward, without a group. It left them weaker, more helpless, more isolated. It left them alone.

I've read a good deal of the commentary on the Million Man March; it quickly became a kind of cottage industry, grist for academics, journalists, sociologists, even for self-proclaimed experts in estimating the size of crowds. It seems to me that all these people must have seen a much more complicated and nuanced event than the one I saw. To me it all seemed so obvious and simple.

A lot of intellectuals — and the vast majority of newspaper columnists, including the kerfuffling grandees of my newspaper and the *New York Times* and the rest of the elite press — seemed not to have seen even an inch past the controversial man who brought us all together that day. Is he a real anti-Semite, they asked again and again, or does he just sound like one? Was his speech a bizarre excursion into numerology, they all wanted to know, or did it just sound like one? People who disagreed with Farrakhan on everything in the world were quick to agree with his assertion that you can't possibly separate the organizer of the event from the event itself — and so, in their automatic condemnation of him, they also automatically and finally condemned the march he led.

Arguing with *Post* columnist Richard Cohen the day after the march I pointed out that the whole day had been so peaceful. By way of reply I got only harrumphs. "I knew it would be that way, I knew it all along," he said, muttering something about the crowd's having been self-selected and not really representative. "It doesn't prove a thing."

Well, with no undue disrespect intended toward either the columnists or Farrakhan, you can separate the two. They were in fact distinctly separate, or at least that's how it seemed to me that day. How big was Farrakhan at the Million Man March? From where I stood, he was a speck. Actually, not even a true speck. You had to know that that big structure far in the distance was the stage, and that there were people on it, before you could convince yourself you were seeing even a speck up there delivering a speech.

A lot has been written about Farrakhan's speech and the extent to which it failed to live up to expectations. The truth is that all the speeches were anticlimactic, every single one. The speechifying certainly wasn't the point of our being there. In fact, quite the opposite: The requirement of listening to speeches was the price that a million men paid to be on the Mall that day. This seemed crystal clear to me, something not even in debate. To be warmly welcomed and listened to, or at least politely tolerated, the only real qualifications a speaker needed were to be African American and male. If you were both black and male, then you had the right to speak and the right to be heard. Clarence Thomas can hardly speak before a black audience anywhere in the country, but that day in Washington he would have been heard.

It's not that people didn't pay attention to the speakers. It's not that they didn't hear the words calling for brotherhood and parental responsibility, calling for an end to drug dealing and domestic abuse, calling for political action and spiritual healing. The words were all good. But they weren't central to the event. They were part of the atmosphere, part of the rich tapestry that lay in the background.

The foreground, the point of the whole thing, consisted of the brown-skinned man standing next to me and the darker man on the other side and the light-skinned man in front of me and the man about my color who sidled past on his way to the porta-john with a polite and respectful "Excuse me, brother." The foreground was whatever microcell of the crowd I happened to find myself in at a given moment. I looked around, and I saw the remarkable lack of pathology in the way people were dealing with one another, and I was amazed and heartened. Like water dripping on rock, minute after minute, hour after hour, for days and months and years, repetition has its undeniable effects. It sounds amazing, it sounds even pathetic, but after so many years of being told in a million different ways that black men were first and foremost a problem, I had found myself believing it was true—I subconsciously had accepted, not just in the statistical or probabilistic sense but as a day-to-day reality, that people like me were a problem. That's not something I would have ever said to anyone, or even acknowledged if pressed on it, but the fact is that it's true. I'll bet an awful lot of other men in that crowd had come to accept that same pernicious premise. But now, as a group but also as a million individuals, we were proving it wrong. There was a black man standing next to me and *he wasn't a problem.* There was a black man standing on the other side of me, and *he wasn't a problem either.* This may sound simplistic, but it came as a relief to experience firsthand the reality that we are not fated to be anybody's problem, not even our own.

In the end, the march was to me a simple statement: Here we are. Whether we represent your hopes or your fears, here we are, uncountable thousands of us, and we're an indelible part of America. We must deal with ourselves, but you must deal with us, too.

I THOUGHT ABOUT race and color that October day in Washington. I looked at the light-skinned brothers and the medium-skinned brothers and the dark-skinned brothers, and I thought about how fervently many people in America wished that race would just go away. And I hoped against all hope that it wouldn't—at least not just yet.

Acknowledgments

THIS BOOK NEVER COULD HAVE BEEN WRITTEN WITHOUT THE assistance, forbearance, and understanding of my family—Avis, Aaron, and Lowell—whose support and encouragement kept me going. My parents, Harold and Louisa Robinson, and my sister, Ellen Robinson, showed me overgenerous measures of faith and pride that I have tried my best to deserve. My late grandmother, the inimitable Sadie Smith, gave me a lifetime's worth of inspiration; my colleagues at the *Washington Post* sent me away on adventures that opened my mind. Many thanks to my agent, Denise Stinson, without whose help this project would not have been possible, and my editor, Paul Golob, who gently forced me to reach far down inside myself and pull out a book. To all, my deepest gratitude.